HIDDEN SPRING

SECOND EDITION

HIDDEN SPRING
The Spiritual Dimension of Therapy

THOMAS HART

Fortress Press

Minneapolis

HIDDEN SPRING:
The Spiritual Dimension of Therapy

Cover design: Jessica Thoreson
Cover photo: Photodisc
Author's photo: Bonjour

The Library of Congress cataloged the first edition of this work as follows:
Hart, Thomas N.
    Hidden spring: the spiritual dimension of therapy/by Thomas Hart.
       p.   cm.
    Includes bibliographical references.
    ISBN 0-8091-3500-0 (pbk):
       1. Psychotherapy—Religious aspects—Christianity. I Title.
RC489.R46H37   1994

                      94-19335
616.89'14—dc20   CIP

The paper used in this publication meets the minimum requirements of American National Standard for Information Sciences—Permanence of Paper for Printed Library Materials, ANSI Z329.48-1984.

Manufactured in the U.S.A.

07   06   05   04   03   02   1   2   3   4   5   6   7   8   9   10

Contents

Preface

A hundred years ago, Sigmund Freud's pioneering ideas opened a new field of human investigation. Modern psychology was born, and it has proved to be a great contributor to human welfare. But, in an unfortunate development, Freud set his face against religion. He regarded it as pure superstition and neurosis, a major impediment to human maturing. Consequently religion and psychology have dwelt in separate worlds, suspicious of one another and not always respectful.

As this new century gets underway, we find ourselves in a quite different situation. Generally speaking, religion and psychology have become mutually respectful, and a fresh and lively dialogue between them seeks to discover what each can learn from the other. Religion began borrowing psychological insights decades ago. Today, psychology is much more open to what religion has to offer it. And a growing number of clients in counseling and psychotherapy want to discuss spiritual concerns in their therapy, simply because spirituality, which embraces everything, is a very important part of their lives.

I believe psychology and spirituality have a lot to offer one another, and that the time for full integration and collaboration has come. Psychology's search for human healing, growth, and fulfillment can be aided tremendously by spirituality, which seeks the same goals but in more ultimate terms. The eminent Swiss psychiatrist, Carl Jung, showed an understanding deeper than Freud's when he called the world's religious traditions "the great psychotherapeutic symbol systems of humankind." Sound spirituality is itself therapeutic, and from its commitment to fulness of life it supports every therapeutic effort. At the same time psychology harbors insights and instruments useful in the attainment of spirituality's goals. These two human endeavors have the resources both to enrich and to critique each other in helpful ways.

1

When I speak of *therapy* or *psychotherapy* in this book, I mean any helping relationship in which a trained professional works with another person who seeks some resolution to problems he or she is experiencing—some healing, liberation, or growth. The word *counseling* could just as well be used. I include psychotherapy of every kind—psychodynamic, humanistic, solution-focused, cognitive/behavioral, systemic, to name a few. I draw on many therapeutic modalities in my own work, and I see all of them as compatible with the explicit inclusion of spirituality in dealing with people and their concerns.

By *spirituality* I mean the way one lives out one's faith in daily life, the way a person relates to the ultimate conditions of existence. There are many spiritualities. The one I know best and will be describing is Christian. I live within the Roman Catholic tradition of Christianity, but I think the broad principles I set forth would be acceptable to most Christians and perhaps even many non-Christians, with whatever translation may be necessary into terms more familiar to each person.

In what follows I place therapy in a spiritual framework, and I draw out the spiritual dimension of the human struggles with which therapy deals. I begin by talking about how Mystery is present and active in all that concerns us. Next, I describe the relationship between psychology and spirituality. I conclude this overview by offering ten principles for a healthy spirituality. The second and longer section of the book is more concrete, showing in six stories of actual counseling how spirituality and psychology merge in practice. My main emphasis is on the practical, for, while many books describe the relationship in theory, few show how to work with the spiritual dimension in the actual practice of counseling.

I write with three different readerships in mind. First as seminarians, pastors, and pastoral counselors. They all receive some training in psychology and therapeutic techniques. The problem is that in counseling sessions psychology often comes to the fore while spirituality is almost forgotten. The two really belong together, particularly in pastoral hands. I write also for people trained strictly in psychotherapy or social work who wish they could dialogue with clients more comfortably about the spiritual dimension of their lives. I write finally for persons who are undergoing therapy and want to understand better how their present struggles can be contextualized within the larger frame of their ultimate destiny.

A word about myself. I grew up in a large Roman Catholic family that took its faith very seriously. I entered the Jesuits at the age of eighteen and began a long course of studies to become a priest. It was not just a course of studies I embarked upon but a form of monastic life. We took vows of poverty, chastity, and obedience, and lived in communities in which growth in the spiritual life and service to others were the core commitments. A ministry that emerged for me even before I was ordained some thirteen years later was that of spiritual direction, a form of one-on-one counseling in which the focus is spiritual growth. When, after twenty-one years as a Jesuit, I left the community and married, I realized I would need another credential to carry on my ministry of counseling. So I earned a master's degree in psychotherapy and have now been in clinical practice for twenty-five years. Today people call me a therapist, though they used to call me a spiritual director. But in practice, I am still doing much the same thing, perhaps with a bit more sophistication, that is, talking with people about their lives and bringing psychological and spiritual perspectives to bear on their concerns. I also earned a doctorate in theology and have continued to teach theology and spirituality to graduate students preparing for ministry. The combination of teaching and counseling keeps me reflecting almost daily on the interaction between psychological and spiritual issues.

One day at a continuing education event that I was teaching for therapists, a pastoral counselor, well-versed and long experienced in the many modalities of psychotherapy, remarked to me that he still thought the best thing we have to offer those who come to us for help is spirituality. The remark really resonated with me. It is true. But the spirituality has to be integrated. And from that conviction flows all that follows.

Part One

GUIDING PRINCIPLES

1.

The Presence of God in Ordinary Life

One of the most common mistakes we make where religion or spirituality are concerned is to think of them as a realm apart, an area of interest to some but not to all, an extracurricular activity without vital bearing on the practical business of daily living. This view is what makes it so easy for psychotherapy, and other fields of human endeavor, to ignore spirituality altogether. My particular concern in this book is to show how God is present and active in the therapeutic project whether we advert to it or not; but to elucidate that I have to begin on a much larger canvas. In this first chapter, I write as a theologian, sharing and grounding a vision of the presence of God in all of life. I want to show that God is more with us than we usually realize, and that we have more religious experience than we ordinarily acknowledge. Out of this larger picture of the relationship between God and ourselves at all times, I will focus in on the particular domain of therapy.

Let me begin with a story. It is a true story, that of Helen Keller, who became blind and deaf when she was two years old. Helen might have lived her whole life consigned to the severe limitations of a person who could not learn. But she had a teacher, caring and creative, who could not put to rest a dream of deeper possibilities. Realizing that touch was the only channel she had into Helen's inner world, this woman devised a crude set of hand motions and, day after day, putting her hand in Helen's, spelled for her the names of things they were experiencing. For a long time, Helen could not make the association between what she was experiencing and the movement in her hand. She only knew that among the many things intruding on her sense of touch there was also this hand constantly moving in hers. That was all. It had no more meaning to her than the walls she bumped into or the wind she felt. Then one day, as Helen was washing her hands at an outdoor pump, this indefatigable mentor signed "water" again and again with a certain desperateness into her hand, and Helen finally got it. She understood that the movements in her hand were more than mere motions. They were *signs*, pointing to the

7

objects of her experience. Thus Helen caught the concept of language, and the doors swung open to the whole realm of human knowledge. From that day forward, she never ceased to educate herself, and her horizon just kept expanding.

Very few people are born with Helen Keller's handicaps, but do we really see and hear? I would assert that we are hardly less blind and deaf than she much of the time. We make the same mistake, thinking the ordinary stuff of our experience is all that there is, failing to see and hear the mystery to which it all points. There is someone signing in our hand too, and we don't get it. Like Helen, we think reality is mere object and motion, when in fact it is all language and communication—God, the mystery in the background, speaking to us through all things.

It is the biblical vision of reality I here attempt to convey. The psalmist puts it this way:

> The heavens are telling the glory of God;
> and the firmament proclaims God's handiwork.
> Day to day pours forth speech,
> and night to night declares knowledge (Ps 19).

> O God, how manifold are your works!
> In wisdom you have made them all;
> the earth is full of your creatures.
> Yonder is the sea, great and wide,
> which teems with things innumerable,
> living things both small and great (Ps 104).

In a vision of faith, all reality is God's creation. And creation, we observe, is a never-ending evolution. What now exists did not spring into being in an instant, but only very gradually took form. That means the divine work continues. God still labors over the world, expressing self in ongoing creativity, and drawing all things toward the purposes for which they are made.

This kind of seeing is the basis of that reverent attitude toward all things which is called contemplation. High in the mountains, amid the snows, we awaken to a sense of the divine presence and feel awe at the grandeur of God. Fishing on a lake, we experience it again.

Spring, with its outpouring of blossoms, proclaims it anew. We sight the hovering hummingbird, or catch a whale breaching the waters. We halve a head of cabbage and really see its folds. A baby is born, and we cradle it in reverent arms. In all these things, God is speaking the divine self, extending self for relationship. Our response, instinctive, is awe, gratitude, worship. In the wonderful words of e. e. cummings, "now the ears of our ears awake, and now the eyes of our eyes are opened." Contemplation is nothing more than this—the awareness of the God-presence in all things.

God's activity is still broader. Love comes into our lives. Someone appreciates us, reflects back to us our goodness and beauty, helps us to see that we ourselves are part of the divine manifestation. God lives in us, too, loving and quietly creating, cocreating with our indispensable help the person we can be. And broader still, all that we actively engage in in life (our work, our loves, our interests, our plea-sures), and all the forces that impinge on us whether we want them to or not (others' ways with us, the blows of misfortune, the many influ-ences of nature and culture)—even when these are not exactly what God would have them be—are instruments of God's creative work. There is divine activity and communication in all of it, and all is opportunity for us, awaiting our response. On that response hinges what we shall make of ourselves.

Metaphors for God's Presence

Several contemporary theologians have tried to awaken us to the spir-itual dimension of our daily situation by offering us metaphors for the divine presence. These metaphors are images drawn from common human experience which help us to see more clearly and feel more palpably how God is present and active in all things.

Roman Catholic theologian Karl Rahner calls God the *horizon* of all experience.[1] For Rahner, God is always at the edges of human awareness, in the same way the horizon is always at the edges of visu-al perception. We do not usually look directly at the horizon, but we see everything against the backdrop it provides. Similarly, we do not directly see God, but God is the backdrop against which we see everything else, and thus God is always at the periphery of our con-sciousness. Rahner amplifies this particularly with regard to two constant activities of the human spirit, questioning and questing. We are always asking questions because we are always wondering. The young child is the perfect example of this activity, by which he wears his parents out. But the wondering persists long after childhood. And we are never fully satisfied with the answer we are given. Every answer simply generates a deeper question. Why this endless wondering? Rahner wonders. Our very questions are our relationship to God, he answers. Each one presses more deeply into the horizon, still unsatisfied, still wanting more of the infinite mystery. Our endless questioning is ever pointed toward the horizon and testifies to our essential relationship to it. As adults we can pursue learning in any realm and we soon discover that all the professors and all the libraries in the world will never put our questions to rest. Our mind's yearning for truth is infinite.

The same dynamic operates in the realm of the human quest. We seek happiness, satisfaction, fulfillment—call it what you will. But nothing satisfies us in the realm of the good either. The child longs to grow up, believing that happiness begins then. But does it? Does it begin with a college degree? Alas, no. A well-paying job? That's great, but it still leaves much to be desired. Perhaps the answer is marriage, sex, intimacy. Hmm. Not all they're cracked up to be. Children, perhaps? Owning our own home? Still unfulfilled. Is it when the kids are raised and gone? Perhaps retirement....The quest stretches on, and all the big milestones prove to be but partial satisfactions soon taken for granted, while our spirit longs restlessly for something more. For our projects, like our questions, prove to be so many arrows fired at the horizon, unsatisfied with everything they hit short of it. As with the true, so with the good: our spirit has an essential relationship with some infinite horizon, right in the midst of our daily engagement with the mundane. Against that ever-present horizon, the limitedness of everything is starkly silhouetted. *Something* of what we seek (God) is contained in every truth and every good—but never enough. Rahner's metaphor of the horizon serves nicely to remind us how present God is to us in all our experience.

A twentieth-century Protestant theologian, Paul Tillich, uses a different but equally compelling metaphor to call attention to the God hidden and revealed in our world. God, Tillich says, is the *depth* in things.[2] If the word "God" means nothing to you, he says, think about where you experience depth in your life. That is where you encounter God, for God is the depth dimension of all reality. It might be in the beauty of a rose really seen. It might be in the goodness of food. It could be in the profound puzzlement of existence. Or the deep joy of being loved. It could be in the agony of feeling alone. Or the sweeping power of great music. Or the passion of a commitment, or any other experience of psychic depth. Where we touch depth, Tillich says, we touch God. His is a marvelous metaphor, because it takes hold of our religious gaze, so often directed upward, and redirects it down and into. For Tillich, God is here, *inside* all things.

Rosemary Radford Ruether uses yet another metaphor to heighten awareness. A feminist theologian mindful of the destructiveness of the arbitrary masculinizing of God, Ruether changes what she sees to be the prevalent God-image, "God the paternal superego," to that of *"God the empowering matrix."*[3] We are thoroughly familiar with God as father, and only slightly less familiar with God as judge (superego), likewise a masculine image. Ruether seeks a more liberating metaphor, truer to our experience of God's goodness and support of us. A matrix, derived from the Latin word for mother, is the ground in which things are embedded or within which they are contained. In this maternal metaphor, Ruether envisions God as the fertile seedbed in which we and all other things are rooted. God not only gives being and life, but keeps serving as the empowering source of growth and development. There is kinship between Ruether's and Tillich's metaphors, in that both see God deep down, God the wellspring or vital source.

Sally McFague, deeply convinced that we must rename God if we want to save the earth, suggests several metaphors to replace God as cosmic monarch and Lord of hosts: God as mother, God as lover, God as friend. All three of them emphasize love, and invite a different sort of relationship with God. Then McFague adds a metaphor for earth: *earth as the body of God.*[4] She seeks to reinvigorate our ancestors' profound sense of earth as charged with the holy. Metaphorically speaking, earth is God's own body. McFague's image derives from religious experiences similar to those of Tillich and Ruether: God the depth in things or God the empowering matrix now extrapolated a bit to God incarnate in the body of the earth.

Charlene Spretnak shows similar thinking in her designation of the world as *Earthbody*. She says it best herself:

> The central understanding in contemporary Goddess spirituality is that the divine—creativity in the universe, or ultimate mystery—is laced throughout the cosmic manifestations in and around us. The divine is immanent, not concentrated in some distant seat of power, a transcendent sky-god. Instead of accepting the notion in patriarchal religion that one must spiritually transcend the body and nature, it is possible to apprehend divine transcendence as the sacred whole, or the infinite complexity of the universe. The Goddess, as a metaphor for divine immanence and the transcendent sacred whole, expresses ongoing regeneration with the cycles of her Earthbody and contains the mystery of diversity within unity: the extraordinary range of differentiation in forms of life on Earth issued from her dynamic form and are kin.[5]

Elaborating on this metaphor, Spretnak offers a compelling vision:

> ...our Neolithic, and probably even our Paleolithic, ancestors perceived the bountiful manifestations of the Earth as emanating from a fertile body—an immense female whose tides moved in rhythm with the moon, whose rivers sustained life, whose soil/flesh yielded food, whose caves offered ritual womb-rooms for ceremonies of sacred community within her body, whose vast subterranean womb received all humans in burial. It is not difficult to understand why they held Her sacred.[6]

All these varied metaphors, based in human religious experience, help to dispel the persistent notion that God is above us or out there somewhere dwelling in a space apart. They are at one in insisting that God is *right here*: the horizon of all experience, the depth in things, the empowering matrix, the dynamic personal soul of Earthbody. That God is in the stuff of our daily experience is hardly a twentieth-century discovery, but it is a truth with a penchant for escaping notice.[7] There is a wonderful little story from the Orient chronicling the recurrent disorientation:

> "Excuse me," said a young ocean fish to an older fish. "Can you direct me to what they call the Ocean? I've been searching everywhere."
> "The Ocean," said the older fish, "is what you are swimming in now. This is it!"
> "This?" said the young fish, disappointed. "This is only water. I'm looking for the Ocean." And he swam away to continue his search.

The Scriptural Basis for a Contemplative Vision of All Reality

These contemporary metaphors for God's presence are indeed thought provoking. But many Christians will ask: Is there any *biblical* basis for thinking this way?

Indeed there is. It would be very strange to find theologians of any age proposing metaphors which lacked scriptural support. The metaphors are freshly coined, it is true, and in that sense non-biblical. But they are consistent with the biblical perception. The reason theologians mint new metaphors is that every age needs fresh insight and articulation to help it relate to God, metaphors closely connected with its life experience. The Bible is, after all, a very ancient book. But the use of metaphors to speak of the experience of God is as old as the Bible itself; even older, as it runs through all the religions of the world.

The criterion for evaluating the validity of fresh metaphors for God is, Does the vision they embody correspond with the biblical vision? More specifically for our purposes here, Does the Bible portray God as somehow a part of everyday experience, as present and interactive with us in the midst of daily life? It does. We can illustrate by drawing on Paul, John, and Jesus.

Paul, who sought to convert the Greeks to Christianity, strolled around the city of Athens one day taking stock of the religious monuments. He saw altars erected to honor countless gods, and, while he was not a polytheist, agreed with the basic religious conviction he saw expressed in these constructions. It was plain that for the Greeks, life was shot through with the divine presence and activity. They saw a god in the fields and the grain on which they depended, another god in the bountiful waters, a god in the mystery of sexuality, a god in the sun and moon and stars, a god at the center of domestic life, and so on. The cosmos was theophany (i.e., divine revelation) to them, a thing of mystery and power permeated with the holy, and everywhere in life it was with divinity that they dealt. Paul agreed with the basic vision, and so he opened his sermon with a declaration of common ground:

> "People of Athens, I see that in every respect you are very religious. As I walked around looking at your shrines, I even discovered an altar inscribed 'To a God Unknown.' Now what you are thus worshiping without knowing it, I intend to make known to you" (Acts 17: 22–23).

So he joins them in their experience of the omnipresence of the divine, and uses the altar to a god unknown to begin to speak of the God in whom he believes. He simply wants to unify their polytheism into a monotheism. So he describes the God who creates all things, and gives breath and life and everything else to human beings. Then he comes back to the original theme of omnipresence:

> "People were to seek God, yes to grope for God, and perhaps eventually to find God—*though God is not really far from any of us, for 'in God we live and move and have our being*,' as some of your own poets have said" (Acts 17:27–28. Italics ours).

Thus Paul finds his own core religious conviction in their religious sources, and quotes it from there to join with them. The conviction is: We are intimately involved with God all the time, for in God we live and move and have our being. From this we can see that Paul's is clearly an *integrated* vision of sacred and secular, a worldview in which the supposedly secular realm is really a sacred realm—for those who have the eyes to see. This is very different from the notion, not uncommon among Christians even today, that God is a being out there somewhere, beyond the visible realm, a God to be called out to and persuaded to come and intervene in what concerns us. Paul's vision suggests that when Christians pray, we ought not to look *up* from our situation, but to look more intently *into* it, for God is already present and active there.

Another place where Paul speaks of this integrated vision is in Romans, where he says:

> "In fact, whatever can be known about God is clear to them (unbelievers): God made it so. Since the creation of the world, invisible realities, God's eternal power and divinity, have become visible, recognized through the things God has made. Therefore these people (unbelievers) have no excuse. They certainly had knowledge of God, yet they did not glorify God or give thanks" (Rm 1:19–21).

Here too, creation is theophany (i.e., God's self-revelation), the basis of that contemplative perspective on all things which moves us to wonder and worship. The text invites us to find God by looking more intensely at and seeing more deeply into our earthly situation.

Consistent with this is Paul's vision of how we should *worship* God. Having completed the lengthy doctrinal part of Romans, Paul comes to the matter of worship.

> "And so, sisters and brothers, I beg you, through the mercy of God, to offer your *selves* as a living sacrifice holy and acceptable to God, your *spiritual* worship. Do not conform yourselves to this age, but be transformed by the renewal of your mind so that you may judge what is God's will, what is good, pleasing, and perfect" (Rm 12:1–2. Italics ours.)

The text literally says offer your *bodies* as a living sacrifice, but as New Testament scholar Rudolph Bultmann points out, Paul means *self* when he uses the term "body" in such contexts.[8] The meaning of the passage is that it is not mainly with religious rites but with our *selves*, or our *whole lives*, that we worship God. Worship is not a separate religious activity, but a spiritual way of living which flows, as Paul explains in the passage, from a radical *metanoia* or conversion— a transformation of our vision and a reorientation of our values to correspond with God's. It stands to reason that if God is present to us in all reality, our response to God would be similarly pervasive of our entire existence.

In John, we find a very similar characterization of true worship. In John's gospel, Jesus says to a woman of Samaria:

> "Believe me, woman, an hour is coming when you will worship the Father neither on this mountain nor in Jerusalem....An hour is coming, and is already here, when authentic worshipers will worship the Father in spirit and truth. Indeed, it is just such worshipers the Father seeks. God is spirit, and those who worship God must worship in spirit and truth" (Jn 4:21–24).

A passage in his first letter broadens this perspective further, portraying John's sense of the pervasive presence of God in our midst. It is one of scripture's best loved places:

> Beloved, let us love one another, because love is of God; everyone who loves is begotten of God and has knowledge of God. The person without love has known nothing of God, for God is love....No one has ever seen God. Yet if we love one another, God dwells in us, and God's love is brought to perfection in us....God is love, and those who abide in love abide in God and God in them (1 Jn 4:7–16).

The beauty of this passage for those who desire contact with God is its attestation that our basic human experience of loving and being loved is itself an experience of God, because human love is suffused with the divine. It is God's love that is operative in us when we love each other. Thus we give God to, and receive God from, one another in our human loving, which puts ordinary love in a remarkable light. There seem to be many people who do not think of themselves as spiritual, yet who show much love in their relationships. This passage blesses them with the good news that they know God better than they think—that they are, in fact, children (begotten) of God.

John's words tie directly into one of Jesus' major parables, his story of the last judgment (Mt 25), in which the criterion of God's judgment of the ultimate worth of a human life is the way the person responds to other persons in need—hungry, thirsty, without shelter, sick, imprisoned. This means that as far as God is concerned, the ultimate criterion is not what we might be inclined to think—orthodox belief or religious activities. No, it is plain human love. What deepens our surprise at Jesus' parable even further is that those who passed the test were not even thinking of God ("When did we see you?") when they acted as they did; they were simply trying to do what was right for the people in need. This is where John gets his inspiration from, since Jesus clearly presents God as intimately involved in our human loving. It is God whom we love when we love the person in need, whether we realize it or not.

This parable exhibits a conviction embedded in all of Jesus' parables: God is present and active throughout the created world. Many are seed parables, which depict the processes of nature as a metaphor for God's hidden but potent activity everywhere. Other natural processes called upon for illustration are the changes of seasons, the action of leaven in dough, trees bearing fruit. Many parables present human beings in interaction, and call attention to the spiritual significance of the choices they make in dealing with one another—armies going to battle, guests at banquets, women working in the home, the elite and their servants, a woman at the collection basket, financiers and debtors, brides and bridegrooms, parents and children, rich people and beggars. Jesus views little children themselves, without further delineation, as a parable of how God wants us to be. It is always ordinary life in which Jesus points to the presence of God.

Now one could say of all this that it is mere illustration, that God is indeed in his distant heaven, and that Jesus, the ingenious storyteller, merely employs the things of this world to indicate what God is *like*. But I would rather suggest that Jesus, out of his profoundly contemplative vision, spoke of seeds, seasons, and persons because he *saw* the Creator's self-manifestion and self-gift right in them. "The reign of God is among you," he declared (Lk 17:21). He vividly felt God's presence and activity in all things, as subsequent mystics have also. For them, earth is holy, the secular is sacred, God is the pulsating energy at the heart of the cosmos.

I want to close this chapter of sources by acknowledging my indebtedness to an historical figure highly influential in mediating the biblical tradition to me—St. Ignatius Loyola, sixteenth-century mystic and founder of the Jesuits. I was myself a Jesuit for twenty-one years, and so drank deeply of Ignatian spirituality. The watchwords of the Ignatian approach to the Christian life are "contemplation in action," and "finding God in all things."

Central to the vision of Ignatius is his profound religious experience of the presence and activity of God in everything. He tries to summarize his experience and lead others into it in the contemplation he places at the very end of his retreat manual, *The Spiritual Exercises*.[9] In this contemplation, Ignatius portrays God not as having created the world, but as creating and animating it constantly; not as having given us the earth as gift, but as giving us, moment to moment, life and breath and every good thing as love-gifts; not as having inscribed the divine signature on the work of art we call earth, but as revealing self constantly in its brimming vitality and offering self through all this for relationship. To accept and enter into this relationship with God is simply to go with the spontaneous response of our hearts: awe, gratitude, love, and the desire to serve God in any way we can for the realization of the divine purpose in the world.

Ignatius believed in prayer as the basis of the Christian life, but he did not believe in spending all day in prayer, even for those who wanted to consecrate their lives entirely to God. He thought the greatest worship we could offer God was to put ourselves at the service of others, and that we could do that in the midst of the world without losing our prayerful contact with God because God was in the world, permeating all things. He thought that the best context for spiritual growth was not in a silent and sequestered space, but in the performance of Christian service, in interaction with others, for there we would be challenged to develop all the virtues. To keep this in focus, he proposed as an essential ingredient in his rather simple prayer program, a twice daily brief examination of conscience, in which we try to discern whether we really are responding to God's invitation in our circumstances. He called this whole way of life "contemplation in action."

I call attention to Ignatius here to round out the catalogue of principal influences on the spirituality I present in this book. That spirituality is biblical to the core, but significantly influenced in its reading of the biblical/theological tradition by process thought, feminist theology, and Ignatian spirituality.

****

This chapter has been an attempt to set forth a vision of faith, and to ground it theologically. The usefulness of the vision is as large as life itself. We begin to live most fully when the ears of our ears awake, and the eyes of our eyes are opened, and we come to know the hidden spring. Everything that will be said about therapy, our more specific focus, is situated within the matrix of this worldview.

2.

Psychotherapy and Spirituality

What is the relationship between psychology and spirituality?

At first glance, they seem to be quite different pursuits. One is a field of science, of fairly recent vintage, seeking to understand the inner and relational dynamics of the human person. The other is rooted in religious experience (some sort of revelation or inspiration), is as old as humankind, and seems most interested in orienting people toward a realm beyond the senses.

From another perspective, the two seem to have a great deal in common. When psychology is put to work in psychotherapy, it endeavors to promote human growth and well-being. But that is a goal it shares with spirituality—even if the two fields might conceive that growth and well-being somewhat differently. Both seek to liberate people from what shackles them, and lead them toward a more fulfilling life. Many counselors today combine a psychological and spiritual orientation. And yet the two fields have not always been friends. Since the days of Sigmund Freud, there has been mutual suspicion, sometimes strong fear and open hostility.

From the side of spirituality, the doubts expressed are these: Isn't therapy sometimes atheistic? Isn't it often merely "humanistic"? Doesn't therapy help people realize themselves in selfish ways, whereas spirituality cultivates personal depth and generates concern for the whole community?[1] Doesn't therapy encourage self-reliance, where what we really need is reliance on God?

From the side of psychology, the counterquestions are: Isn't religion often precisely the greatest impediment to mental health? Doesn't it make people neurotic, preoccupied with guilt and fear? Doesn't it keep them in childish subservience—to religious authorities as well as to some imagined God (Freud's chief criticism)? Doesn't it draw their energies away from life in this world toward some life supposedly to come (Karl Marx's chief criticism)? And doesn't it engender more rigidity, more sectarianism, more hatred and oppression of others than it does love and community, whatever it may profess?

These are sobering questions all, demonstrating how either psychology or spirituality can go astray. They lead in the direction of the only sort of answer about their relationship that will satisfy. Both psychology and spirituality (which is usually housed in organized religion) need to examine themselves and listen to each other to discern whether they really are promoting human well-being: true liberation, health, wholeness, fulfillment.

Toward an Authentic Relationship between Psychotherapy and Spirituality

The etymology of "therapy" is the Greek word *therapeuein*, which means "to heal." Thus therapy is the art of healing. The etymology of "salvation," religious faith's promised reward, the Greek word *soteria* and the Latin word *salus*, which both mean "healing, health, wholeness." This is illuminating. The idea in the two different contexts is exactly the same. Salvation itself is healing or wholeness. In the New Testament, salvation has a much broader sense than the restricted meaning it has acquired in many Christian minds: getting to heaven if you live a good life. It means all the healing, health, and wholeness which come to the person who follows Jesus. Its primary denotation is for this life. "*Today* salvation (healing) has come to this house," Jesus says after his encounter with Zaccheus (Lk 19). "Your faith *has* made you whole," Jesus says to the woman with the hemorrhage (Mk 5). Both therapy and spirituality aim to bring healing and wholeness to the person in this lifetime.

Coming at the same matter from the problem side, when people seek therapy, they do it because they feel unhappy about something, and cannot find their way to peace. But that is exactly why people also seek help from religion. A remarkable recent book about the religious quest is Antony Fernando and Leonard Swidler's *Buddhism Made Plain: An Introduction for Christians and Jews.*[2] Fernando is a Roman Catholic professor with doctorates in both Buddhism and Christian theology. Swidler is also a Roman Catholic, and a theologian deeply schooled in both Jewish and Christian thought. They collaborate to show that there is a remarkable inner affinity among these three great religions: all have the same aim—the liberation of the human person. In their original inspiration, all three envisioned a this-worldly liberation rather than life after death. Each of the founding geniuses looked at the human predicament and fashioned a path of liberation or salvation. The paths differ in some respects, each much influenced by the culture in which it was crafted. Yet they are at one not only in their goals, but also in the fundamental values to which each invites commitment so that liberation or salvation can be realized. Those values are honesty, self-acceptance, kindness, humility, tolerance, hope, self-control, material simplicity, sharing of goods, service of others, forgiveness, serenity, non-violence, contemplation. These are the values on which the liberated, enlightened, or saved life of the individual and the whole community must be based.

Would therapy quarrel with any of those values, or challenge the idea that those who cultivate them lead an enlightened, liberated, healthy life? It is hard to imagine it doing so. For therapy, too, espouses liberation, healing, and wholeness. Therapy, too, seeks to foster liberation from inner and outer conflict, self-acceptance, satisfying relationships with others, acceptance of reality and constructive engagement with it, a basic sense of security and inner peace, and the fullest flowering of personal possibilities. Would a sound spirituality quarrel with any of these goals of therapy? That, too, is hard to imagine. In the end, then, are there not ample grounds for spirituality and psychology to be good friends and collaborators?

Why then have they come into conflict with one another? Because both sometimes fall short of what they can and ought to be. When therapy makes people more selfish instead of more loving, it is poor therapy. When therapy is closed to God, it is needlessly and impoverishingly constricted. When spirituality fosters neurotic guilt, fear, or dependence, or breeds hatred and oppression of others, it is bad spirituality. Either therapy or spirituality can stray from its true course. When either brings forth fruits of this kind, it stands in need of correction from the better parts of its own tradition as well as from the other endeavor.

In sum, when psychotherapy and spirituality are both sound, they are united in their goal of promoting human well-being. They are not separate realms, and they are certainly not opposed. The best way to think of their relationship is to envision spirituality as the wider frame of meaning, value, and power within which psychotherapy operates. This follows from what we saw in the previous chapter.

Since God is the horizon or depth dimension of *all* experience, then God is the horizon or depth dimension of psychotherapy. Spirituality deals with the ultimate issues, the deepest questions, the foundational meanings and values of human life in general, and therefore of therapy in particular. Therapy needs spirituality's orientations. Spirituality needs therapy's insights and instrumentalities.

I should make it clear that by "spirituality" I mean something slightly different from, yet closely akin to "religion." I mean the fundamental orientation of one's life, one's relationship to the ultimate foundations of existence, what Karl Rahner calls the transcendence of the human spirit. It is true that for most people spirituality is nurtured within the context of organized religion. There it is usually enriched and guided by a whole tradition of sacred writings, holy exemplars, nourishing rituals, helpful teaching and preaching, and the support of a congenial community. But in relation to organized religion, spirituality is both prior and more personal; it is the reason religious organizations come into being. We are spiritual whether or not we belong to a religious denomination. That orientation to something beyond, that questioning and questing, that irrepressible transcendence of the human spirit, and God's self-gift to each of us for a relationship, are simply part of the constitution of our existence, whether we are fully aware of it or not, and whether we cultivate it within the context of organized religion or not.

Psychotheorists Who Recognize the Opening to the Spiritual

There have been many prominent psychotheorists who show a clear sense of those windows where therapy opens out into that larger framework of spirituality within which it lives. I would now like briefly to summarize the thought of several of them, to show how they view the interplay. Let us consider Carl Jung, Viktor Frankl, Abraham Maslow, Robert Kegan, and Gerald May.

Probably the best known of the group, and easily the most invoked when spirituality seeks a sympathetic psychotheorist, is Carl Jung. This eminent Swiss psychiatrist is well known for his keen interest in the spiritual. The basis of his openness was his own religious experiences, which began when he was very young. Though he never affiliated with a church (he was not impressed with organized religion), he retained a lively spiritual sense throughout his life; and when he was asked at the age of eighty whether he believed in God, he replied: "Believe? I don't believe. I *know*." Jung was well aware of Freud's reputation and had learned much from him before they ever met. When they did come together, they hit it off instantly, and had lengthy exchanges on psychological issues. For a period of time they even interpreted one another's dreams. But there was no mistaking Freud's hostility to spiritual considerations, and Jung gradually realized that their friendship would fracture over this fundamental difference. It did. All of this is detailed in Jung's absorbing autobiography, *Memories, Dreams, and Reflections.*[3]

Jung's interest was not in the God out there, but in the God in here, the God of religious experience, the God of the psyche. God is one and the same, but Jung's starting point was not cosmology or ontology but psychology, and it was the psyche's experience of God and the symbols for God found there that intrigued him. Jung began to notice that some of the same symbols and stories of God appeared in widely varying religious cultures, and he devoted many years to the researching of these universal religious symbols, which he called archetypes. Thus, by ever-expanding scholarly interest, the psychiatrist became a comparative religionist. Jung reveals a foot in both camps when he remarks that the world's religions are the great therapeutic symbol systems of humankind.

For Jung, God is active in our lives deep within us, and if we want to live our destiny, we must attune ourselves to this energy deep inside. He emphasized the importance of listening to our dreams as to an avenue of divine communication, a practice found in the Bible itself. He also found a revelatory function in our deep positive or negative emotional stirrings, and even in our daydreams. He remarked that he had dealt with no client in the second half of life whose problem was not at bottom spiritual. For Jung, the domains of the psychological and the spiritual were always interwoven. It seemed to him impossible to drive God out of the psyche.[4]

Viktor Frankl is another well known psychotherapist with an integral sense of the spiritual. Where Freud thought the human being was driven by the desire for pleasure, and Alfred Adler thought we were driven by the desire for personal fulfillment, Frankl was convinced we are driven by the quest for *meaning*.[5] Frankl's position was most profoundly influenced by the years he spent as a Jewish prisoner in the Nazi camps of World War II. There he observed that the people who survived the dreadful hardships were those who maintained some *reason to live* or *meaning* which sustained them.[6] Sometimes it was a beloved person they yearned to return to, or some important work they wished to complete before they died. Sometimes it was a religious faith. Whatever it was, it was the sustaining power which kept them going in a time of immense suffering. Those who lacked this sort of reason to live sooner or later succumbed to the abundant forces of death. Out of this experience Frankl founded his school of "logotherapy" or meaning therapy, in which the therapist works to help clients unearth and name that personal meaning which gives purpose and focus to their existence. Living in fidelity to this meaning is the basis of the person's mental health.

Frankl is aware that at a given time in life, an individual might name pleasure, wealth, security, career, or family as their purpose in life. What he points out is that all of these meanings are provisional: any can be obliterated by events beyond the person's control. Then the person is compelled to dig deeper. Frankl's position is that only a transcendent meaning ultimately holds up to the test of life. This is the point where psychology opens out into spirituality as its necessary fulfillment.

> Religion provides one with more than psychotherapy ever could—and it also demands more of one.[7]

Frankl is convinced that the human person is spiritual at the core, and is an inveterate seeker of ultimate meaning. Each person has to find his or her own meaning. He says we find meaning in being responsible to the many calls which come to us from the particulars of our situation at any given time. Every situation has a call in it, a chance and a challenge to fulfill ourselves by being responsible to it. Frankl agrees with Adler that self-actualization is the goal. But he emphasizes that human existence is always directed to something other than itself, a meaning to fulfill or a person to love. For Frankl, in fact, self-actualization is not an object to be directly sought, but is rather the unintentional by-product of that self-transcendence which being responsible requires. It is conscience that tells us what to do, and conscience is the voice of God within us. Frankl sees religion as the search for ultimate meaning, and holds that there is a religious sense, or latent relationship with God, deeply rooted in every person's unconscious depths.[8] He sounds at times like a theologian.

Commenting specifically on the relationship between psychiatry and religion, Frankl says that they are different *dimensions*. They are by no means mutually exclusive. Because religion is the higher dimension, it includes, subsumes, or encompasses psychiatry. Here his formulation of the relationship very closely resembles my own.

Psychologist Abraham Maslow is probably best known for his schematization of the "hierarchy of human needs." Maslow sees the newborn human being as ideally moving step-by-step up a ladder from the most basic physiological needs (food, drink, shelter) all the way to the highest self-realization needs. He is convinced that you get healthier people if you meet their needs, and healthier people behave better, i.e., are less destructive, selfish, dishonest, etc.[9] His premise is that if you meet a child's physiological needs, safety needs, love needs, and self-esteem needs, the first four on the ladder (the so-called "deficiency needs") the child will naturally move on to the self-actu-alization needs, i.e., becoming most fully a self, realizing personal potentials, growing as a human being. If you do not, the child cannot move on, but is stuck in seeking again and again as an adult to get those basic needs for safety, love, and self-esteem met.

What Maslow found in his study of fully self-actualized or healthy people (those whose needs have been met) was that they are self-accepting and accepting of others and of reality. They are autonomous—free from prejudice, fear of the unknown, and the uncritical acceptance of the various cultural and religious programs that surround them. They generally respect and love people regardless of their education, status, color, religion, etc. They are capable of deeper friendship, and have more peak experiences. They are not self-absorbed, but beamed on something larger than themselves. They do not take the good things of life for granted, but are grateful for them and have a large capacity to enjoy the ordinary things—sunsets, flow-ers, food, sex, children. They may have some bad habits and behave poorly at times, but they are generally estimable people.

Thus Maslow's hierarchy of needs opens out naturally at the top to spiritual values as the full flowering of human development. His survey of traits of fully actualized persons is practically a list of "the virtues" of classical Christian spirituality according to St. Thomas Aquinas. He knows the human spirit's yearning for transcendence, and wrote a special book on *Religions, Values, and Peak Experiences.*[10] Having documented the breadth of human spiritual experience, which for him is clearly not bounded by organized religion, Maslow comments from his standpoint within empirical psychology:

> It is also increasingly developing that leading theologians, and sophisticated people in general, define their god not as a person, but as a force, a principle, a gestalt-quality of the whole of Being, an integrating power that expresses the unity and therefore the meaningfulness of the cosmos, the "dimension of depth," etc. At the same time, scientists are increasingly giving up the notion of the cosmos as a kind of simple machine, like a clock, or as congeries of atoms that clash blindly, having no relation to each other except push and pull, or as something that is final and eternal as it is, and that is not evolving or growing....These two groups seem to be coming closer and closer together in their conception of the universe as "organismic," as having some kind of unity and integration, as growing and evolving and having direction and, therefore, having some kind of "meaning." Whether or not to call this integration "God" finally gets to be an arbitrary decision and a personal indulgence determined by one's personal history, revelations, and myths.[11]

There are echoes in this statement of Rahner, Tillich, Whitehead, Teilhard. Maslow exhibits an openness toward the spiritual which results in an all-embracing synthesis.

There have been efforts on the part of many psychologists in recent decades to map the stages of human growth and development. Among these thinkers, Erik Erikson, Piaget, Kohlberg, Levinson, Vaillant have been at one in making full individual *autonomy* the goal of personal growth. Then a woman's voice was heard, pointing out that these theorists are all men, and show a male bias in their conceptions of personal development. Harvard educationist Carol Gilligan writes specifically of female development, and stresses *relationship* as the goal of personal growth.[12] Perhaps the truth lies in a balanced blend of the two emphases: individual autonomy *and* healthy relationships. Such a balance can be found in the work of Harvard psychologist Robert Kegan.[13] Kegan stresses the need for developing autonomy *and* relationship at every stage from infancy through old age. He points out that true autonomy can neither develop nor be sustained without plenty of healthy relationships, and healthy relating can only happen between two genuinely autonomous individuals.[14]

Once these two essential ingredients of human self-realization are framed by psychology, the link with Christian spirituality immediately suggests itself. Jesus' great commandment—love your neighbor as yourself—envisions a balance of a proper love of self with a generous love of neighbor. Christian spirituality has sometimes so overstressed love of others that it has forgotten to include a proper love of self. But when it does balance the two, it is in harmony with this central psychological insight into the ideal of personal development.[15]

Finally, contemporary psychiatrist Gerald May shows a keen appreciation of the places where therapy opens out into spirituality.[16] He tells how in the early years of his practice he felt profound discouragement because he saw he could not cure people. He realized that healing had to come from beyond himself, from God, and this insight marked the beginning of his own keen interest in spirituality.

May analyzes in particular the widespread problem of addiction in society today—addiction to drugs, sex, work, money, or whatever else. He maintains that we can understand the problem of addiction only if we track it down to its spiritual root. That root is the desire for God, universally present in human beings though often repressed. Addiction is this hunger for God fastened on the wrong object, some false god, to which we give our love, time, energy, "worship." Addiction is the futile attempt to fill the empty space inside us with what cannot fill it and only adds to our troubles. May adds that since any addiction involves loss of willpower, when we are caught in one we cannot extricate ourselves unassisted. Only grace—God's empowering love—can set us free.

May is careful to maintain a balance in his assessment of what breaks the hold of an addiction. It is always a combination of our own best effort and God's gracious empowerment, neither of which can succeed without the other. When the addiction has been let go, the empty space is again evident. There is no cure for that; we must live with it. It is our orientation toward God, who is the true fulfillment of our existence. What we need to do is cultivate a relationship with God through prayer. This endpoint of May's analysis is reminiscent of a remark Freud, in more pessimistic tones, made apropos of the endpoint of psychoanalytic treatment: When we have cured people's neuroses, Freud said, they still have to go out and face all the problems of existence. But where Freud saw darkness, May sees an opening to the spiritual, the only possible answer to our restless quest of ultimate meaning and value.

> There are limits to the psychological universe, and one must go beyond those limits to seek answers to the deepest questions of life.[17]

May's thinking is reminiscent of the philosophy of Alcoholics Anonymous, which also underscores the importance of spiritual resources in helping people recover from addiction. Admitting that one's life has become unmanageable and turning oneself and one's affairs over to a Higher Power, however one understands that, are for AA crucial to breaking the grip of an addiction. AA is a good example of a therapy which relies essentially on spirituality as an ingredient.

This concludes our brief survey of some psychologists who demonstrate psychotherapy's openness to the spiritual. The survey is neither comprehensive, nor is it meant to constitute any sort of proof.[18] But what these thinkers do show is not only the congeniality of values and goals in these two related realms, but the demand for completion which psychology exhibits at many points—completion by that larger and deeper domain within which all things are situated.

Spirituality Good and Bad

If psychology has to be careful not to neglect or, worse, suppress a constituent dimension of the human person, spirituality must also be careful. Let us turn now to the perils that lurk within that realm.

Religion is a dangerous thing. It can do great harm, as well as great good. What makes it dangerous is its immense power, which derives from its appeal to the Absolute or Ultimate as source for what it says and does. Religion signs God's name to what it proclaims, and therefore demands total allegiance. What it fails to acknowledge is that it is often mere human ideas to which it assigns God's authority.

This is patent in a tragedy like Jonestown, where devout believers followed their pastor's directions to the point of poisoning themselves en masse—all in the name of God. But we need not appeal to such an extreme case to make the point. Religions have done great harm throughout history. To take just the Christian instance, Christianity has waged religious wars, persecuted the Jewish people, sanctioned the torture of those who disagreed with its teachings and sentenced many to death, prevented others from practicing their religious traditions and worked to obliterate those traditions where it had the power to do so. In Christianity's holy book, the Bible, one can easily find texts to support many evils, and these texts have often been actually invoked to sanction the following: militarism, racism, sexism, slavery, tyrannical government, homophobia, religious persecution, capital punishment, and the rape of the earth. The Aryan movement appeals to the Bible. So does apartheid. Christian churches themselves appeal to the Bible in support of sexist marriage and the exclusion of women from equal status in the church.[19] More on the individual level, it is not hard to find persons whose religious beliefs are doing them more harm than good, causing more blockage and pain than freedom, joy, or peace.[20] In social situations one encounters people who call themselves "recovering Catholics," and many therapists spend a great deal of time trying to undo the damage done by the churches in the area of sexuality. For our purposes here, the point is that not just any reading of spirituality promotes human well-being, and so not just any reading of spirituality dovetails with the goals of an enlightened therapy.

Instructive in this regard is the testimony of a renowned educator and child psychologist, A. S. Neill, who for some forty years ran an unusual boarding school for children in England.[21] These were kids 5–16 who were not doing well in the educational system. What Neill suspected when he began and was totally convinced of when he finished has a bearing on our concern here with good and bad spirituality.

Neill did not require his charges to attend classes, though a rich variety of classes were held every day. There were abundant play opportunities also. He did not require much work of them; just the housekeeping needed to keep the place going. Policies and rules were agreed upon at community meetings; the same meetings mediated disputes and meted out penalties for offenses. There was one overarching rule: You can do whatever you want here, as long as you do not violate the rights of others.

Under this simple regime, strange and wonderful things happened. At first kids, many of them refugees from convent schools, stayed away from classes; they fully expected to be confronted and coerced, and then they would reengage their accustomed struggle with authority. But there was no confrontation, and before long, whether out of boredom or curiosity, they would join various classes. They also played a lot. They learned to be careful about the rights of others. They pursued their interests, one opening out into another. If they wanted to go on to college, they found out what the requirements were and applied themselves. Many made it.

Neill has some thought-provoking observations:

> The difficult child is the child who is unhappy. He is at war with himself; and in consequence he is at war with the world.

> The difficult adult is in the same boat. No happy man ever disturbed a meeting, or preached a war, or lynched a Negro. No happy woman ever nagged her husband or her children. No happy man ever committed a murder or a theft. No happy employer ever frightened his employees.[22]

Then the question is, where does unhappiness come from, and how do you cure it?

> If the word happiness means anything, it means an inner feeling of well-being, a sense of balance, a feeling of being contented with life. These can exist only when one feels free....Happiness might be defined as the state of having minimal repression. The happy family lives in a home where love abides; the unhappy family in a tense home.[23]

Freedom and repression are major themes in Neill. He believes children are fundamentally good, and will be all right if allowed to live their own inner dynamism without repressions. Children will outgrow their fixations, "bad" habits, even the self-centeredness natural to kids, if they are left unopposed. Neill is wary of organized religion because it emphasizes original sin and fear of punishment, because it imparts so much moral instruction and so facilely labels what is good and bad. Neill's only restraining principle on children was respect for the rights of others in exercising their own rights. This is, after all, Jesus' own golden rule.

For Neill, there are two fundamental stances toward human existence, anti-life and pro-life. He was committed to creating and maintaining an environment for kids that was pro-life. I think we can employ his criteria in evaluating a spirituality.

When I use the word *anti-life*, I do not mean death-seeking. I mean fearing life more than fearing death. To be anti-life is to be pro-authority, pro-church religion, pro-repression, pro-oppression, or at least subservient to these.

Let me summarize: Pro-life equals fun, games, love, interesting work, hobbies, laughter, music, dance, consideration for others, and faith in people. Anti-life equals duty, obedience, profit, and power. Throughout history anti-life has won, and will continue to win as long as youth is trained to fit into present-day adult conceptions.[24]

Pro-life or anti-life: that is the question. In the field of religion, one of the gratifying developments of our day is the growing dialogue among the various traditions of the world. Out of the mutual exchange between Christians, Jews, Hindus, Buddhists, Muslims, and others is being born less arrogance and more respect, the recognition of many common values, more felt need to critique one's own beliefs and behavior, and a willingness to be enriched by others without giving up the essentials of one's own tradition.

As the great religions begin to recognize that from the human encounter with the Transcendent through the ages there have emerged many divergent religious systems all claiming to be based on divine revelation, each has had to admit that *human beings* have had much more to do with the formulation of "divine revelation" than was previously thought. This is not to deny either revelation or inspiration, but simply to recognize that the "word of God" never reaches us unfiltered, but always only through a human recipient/transmitter limited in various ways by the historical/cultural situation in which they encounter the Holy. This explains why all the religions are palpably shaped by the cultures in which they were born. It explains why they vary significantly in the ways they describe the Mystery which transcends understanding, and why even their holy scriptures show an admixture of cultural ignorance and sinful attitudes with the genuine spiritual nourishment they offer.

Out of the dialogue of the religions there has emerged a felt need for some criterion by which authentic and inauthentic religion or religious elements can be distinguished. Without it, any religious teaching or practice has equal claim to legitimacy with any other. The question is not a new one, as the Hebrew scriptures already debated how to discern true from false prophets, and the Christian scriptures reflect the same concern.

In the contemporary discussion among the religions, it is *the human good, individual and collective*, that is invoked as the criterion for judging the authenticity of religious elements.[25] The core conviction is that religion exists to promote human well-being, and that it must always remain open to criticism as to whether it is actually doing that or not. This criterion would be very congenial to Jesus, who spoke up in defense of his disciples that sabbath day they were picking grain from the fields to satisfy their hunger. All work was forbidden on the sabbath. But Jesus said, "The sabbath was made for human beings, not human beings for the sabbath" (Mk 2:27). The human good, individual and collective, is the ultimate norm of authentic religion.

Rosemary Radford Ruether demonstrates how this criterion works when applied specifically to the problem of the oppression of women, an injustice which sometimes appeals to the Bible and long-standing Christian tradition for its validation. Ruether is aware that one of the questions within the Christian feminist movement is whether the Bible, so patriarchal in its attitudes, can be used as a resource for women at all, or must simply be abandoned. Ruether opts for keeping it, but only after naming "a canon within the canon" to serve as a norm for interpretation of the whole. That canon is the prophetic tradition. The prophetic tradition in the Bible, Ruether notes, rejects every elevation of one social group over others as the image and agent of God, and every use of God to justify subjugation.

> Four themes are essential to the prophetic-liberating tradition of biblical faith: 1) God's defense and vindication of the oppressed; 2) the critique of the dominant systems of power and their powerholders; 3) the vision of a new age to come in which the present system of injustice is overcome and God's intended reign of peace and justice is installed in history; 4) finally, the critique of ideology, or of religion, since ideology in this context is primarily religious. Prophetic faith denounces religious ideologies and systems that function to justify and sanctify the dominant, unjust social order.[26]

Noting that no religious group has ever accorded equal authority to all parts of the Bible, Ruether, finding the Bible's highest norm in its own ongoing prophetic critique of any status quo, is able to use the Bible in support of the liberation of women in spite of its endemic sexism. From this foundation she develops her feminist critical principle:

> Theologically speaking, whatever diminishes or denies the full humanity of women must be presumed not to reflect the divine or an authentic relation to the divine, or to reflect the authentic nature of things, or to be the message or work of an authentic redeemer or a community of redemption.[27]

I develop this at length not only because the liberation of women from oppression is at the heart of much therapeutic work with individuals and couples, but also because Ruether's principle has an even broader application than that. Substitute "any person" for "women" in the above quotation, and you still have an unassailable principle, whether "any person" be a person of color, a gay or lesbian person, a Marxist, a street person, a child, an elderly person, a prisoner, or a whole nation or continent of persons. What denies or diminishes their full humanity is not of God, the right order of things, or a community of redemption. What affirms and promotes their full humanity is of God, the right order of things, and a community of redemption. Whether we draw this norm from the Bible or from common sense and an instinctive reverence for persons, we can bring it to the Judeo/Christian or any other religious tradition and say: "I will not accept as from God anything you proclaim or practice which violates this fundamental norm." The criterion is pragmatic, in the sense that it judges religious elements (doctrines, scriptures, laws, rituals, persons) by what they produce in practice. This is the criterion Jesus himself offered for distinguishing true and false prophets: "By their fruits you will know them" (Mt 7:20). How far we are from realizing this stated ideal in practice is seen in the many kinds of "hate crimes" and sectarian wars still rife in the world today. At least we have the growing dialogue of the religions, and some consensus on the true purpose of religion.

The Question of Humanism

Humanism has a bad name among some Christians, and anything bearing the label is rejected out of hand as opposed to faith. This is a curious attitude. It is important to be clear about what humanism is. The term basically means an attitude or way of life centered on human interests and values. That does not seem to be a bad thing. It has long been understood that when people undertake a program of humanistic studies, they are devoting themselves to the great classics of civilization, in quest of the good, the true, and the beautiful. The hoped-for outcome of this exposure to large quantities of great literature, philosophy, and art, is that the student be inspired to the better life, the higher life, goodness and virtue. Humanism is thus an interest in the genuine human good.

In this sense of the term, every religion is a "humanism," for every religion is centered on human interests and values, and seeks the human good. Why would it be of any interest to us otherwise? Moses, Jesus, Gautama, Muhammad were all humanists. Their concern was to serve the interests of human living, to show us how to live in ways that realize meaning and value for ourselves and others.

Why, then, the antipathy to "humanism" among some Christians? Partly because of a misunderstanding of what humanism is, but partly, too, because there have been atheistic as well as theistic humanisms in the history of civilization. It would seem to make sense that Christians reject atheistic humanism. But even this is risky, since there is much that is sound and true in various atheistic humanisms, e.g., the Freudian, the Marxist, the Buddhist. Many of the values espoused in these systems correspond with Christian values. In dialogue with their adherents, we always have much to learn, or at least to agree with. Particularly if we come to know the social context in which each of these atheistic humanisms arose, we can understand why their proponents felt impelled to react against the sort of religious attitudes prevalent in their cultures. They seem to have thought that the only way to liberate people from the negative elements of the cultural religion was to throw out the religion altogether and become "atheistic." We may need to hear what they were rejecting and why, so that we can purify our own belief and practice of false and harmful elements. Religion is a dangerous thing, always in need of reform. The ultimate norm by which we must critique every religion, as well as every humanism and ideology, is that of the genuine human good, individual and communal.

****

What I have tried to show here, with the assistance of several psychotheorists and theologians, is that a sound psychotherapy and a sound spirituality are united in their goal of promoting human growth and well-being. They are not separate realms, and certainly not opposed realms; they exhibit extensive overlap. God is the depth-dimension of all experience, and so spirituality is the broader context within which psychotherapy operates, dealing specifically as it does with the ultimate values, hopes, and power (God's creative and saving love) by which we orient ourselves. At many points psychology instinctively reaches out toward spirituality for its completion. At the same time, psychology serves spirituality with its insights into psychodynamics and its instrumentalities for promoting liberation and growth. Both psychotherapy and spirituality stand in permanent need of critique, from the best of their own traditions as well as from each other, as to whether they are being true in promoting the goal: the genuine human good, individual and communal.

3.

Toward a Healthy Spirituality: Ten Guiding Principles

People come to therapy because something is bothering them. They begin, not by talking about God, but by talking about their problem. What they seek are solutions, and ultimately relief from the suffering they are experiencing.

So their immediate concerns must be addressed in a practical way. But spirituality, too, is relevant, suggesting a way of looking at the problem, and pointing to some of the key values present in the situation. It offers a way of thinking about how God is already present with the person in the struggle, and how they might best respond to the challenge they are facing.

In the last chapter, we examined the broad relationship of psychology and spirituality. Here we look at ten principles of a healthy Christian spirituality which speak directly to the typical struggles of human existence, and which give therapy an orientation. These principles represent my core faith convictions, and I find myself regularly articulating one or other of them in therapy because they have direct and very practical relevance to what a client and I are discussing. They flow logically from the theological foundations of the preceding two chapters.

1. God wants life for us.

This is the first and most important principle of the series, because it names God's fundamental stance. God is for us. God stands on the side of life and of all that belongs to life—liberation, healing, expansion, well-being, growth, joy. As the eminent Roman Catholic theologian Edward Schillebeeckx puts it, "the human cause is God's cause."[1]

In support of this contention, we might cite particular biblical texts. But the overarching proof is the entire biblical narrative, in which, from first to last, God is laboring for humanity's good. We call the entire account "salvation history," because it is a string of stories of rescue. First from primeval chaos, then from a state of slavery, then from being lost, then from hunger, then from opposing armies, God keeps saving people. God gives land. God gives direction (the Law) as to the purpose of human life and the kind of behavior that supports life for all. When, over time, powerful individuals oppress the people, God sends prophets to confront the oppressors so as again to set the people free. Jesus stands within this prophetic tradition, aligns himself with the poor and oppressed of society, confronts the wealthy and powerful, and spends himself in a ministry of healing and liberation in God's name. The moral of the whole biblical story is that God wants life for us. God's stance could hardly be clearer.

At the head of the book stands an image so placed because it is cardinal. It is the image of a man and a woman in a lovely garden which has been given them for their enjoyment, with minimal stipulations for their safety. The whole of God's purpose is epitomized in this portrait (Gen 1–2). It is as if God said: "It's all for you. Enjoy it."

Isaiah describes God's love this way: "Can a mother forget her infant, be without tenderness for the child of her womb? Even should she forget, I will never forget you. See, upon the palms of my hands I have written your name"(Is 49:15–16).

Jesus' words are these:

"I have come that they might have life, and have it to the full" (Jn 10:10).

"If God is for us, who can be against?" Paul asks (Rm 8:31).

John sums it up in three words: "God is love" (1 Jn 4:8).

Why lay stress on this point, so massively attested? Because Christians themselves have such difficulty really believing it. We are afraid to get mixed up with God because we fear God will take everything away from us! Christian spirituality itself has been the culprit in some of its representations, teaching that we should love the cross, that the harder thing is the better thing, that God sends us sufferings as a special mark of love. Jesus never said any of this. Where he saw suffering, he moved to alleviate it. His dedication was to the cause of life. People sometimes think therapy promotes self-actualization and personal fulfillment, whereas spirituality looks askance at such goals. I emphasize this fundamental principle of spirituality to make it clear that God, too, stands on the side of self-actualization and personal fulfillment.

When in therapy, then, people seek to free themselves from the damage of their past, to find their true selves, or to grow into the fullness of their possibilities, their purpose is aligned with God's purpose, and the energies of God support their efforts. To put it another way, where healing, reconciliation, liberation, wholeness, and love are happening, God's purpose is being realized.

2. The purpose of our life is to learn how to love.

Near the end of his public life, Jesus is asked what the greatest of God's commandments is. He sums up the whole Bible and all his own teaching with what we have come to call The Great Commandment: Love God with your whole heart, and love your neighbor as yourself (Mk 12:28–34). In John's gospel, Jesus offers a slight variation of it: "Love one another as I have loved you" (Jn 13:34). From this we might fairly conclude that the very purpose of our lives is to learn how to love.

Our experience bears this out, telling us how supremely valuable love is—how much we crave it, how satisfied we feel in giving it, how greatly it helps in making life's difficulties more bearable. No wonder Jesus values it so. Our experience also shows us how hard it is to love well. No matter where we are in the life span, we are doubtless still far from loving our enemies, far from taking the welfare of people not in our immediate circle much into account, far alas, even from properly loving those who are closest to us. No wonder Jesus, surveying the human scene, reminds us so frequently that love is the answer.

It is not just others we find it hard to love. We do not usually love ourselves much either, and need a push in that direction. This, too, is part of the commandment, and hence part of our project. Many of us are far harder on ourselves than on anyone else. We criticize ourselves mercilessly, abuse our bodies, shy away from asking for what we need or want, submit meekly to the abuse of others, disquali-

fy ourselves in advance when a job or relationship we would like is
within reach. For many Christians who indeed love others generously,
the hardest part of the commandment is learning to be good to themselves and to receive the love of others.

Every therapeutic issue comes down to love in some way. How
should I deal with my husband or wife? How should we deal with this
child? This parent? Should I stay in this relationship or leave it? Why
do I have no friends? Do I have any value, any rights? These are all
questions about love, I remind people, and love is at bottom a spiritual
issue, the most important issue of your life, the very purpose of it. So
how will you balance a genuine love for others with a genuine love
for yourself? In the choices you make about your life situation, you
are always creating both your own personhood and that of others.
That is surely a spiritual matter.

One particular application of this principle is to the life of the
person who feels empty, or as if their life is meaningless. Often the
problem is that they do not love very much. They are centered on
themselves, and walk the world asking, "Who will love me?" They
need to be turned around, and live from the question, "Who needs
me?" or "Whom can I love?" If they do that they will find more happiness and their life will have meaning. They will get love in return
too. "Give, and it will be given to you," Jesus teaches (Lk 6:38); and
it was obviously the driving principle of his own life. If love is what
we are made for, little wonder there is emptiness if we are not doing
much of it.

In therapy, I find this principle a great motivator. In marriage,
for example, once a couple realizes that learning to love one another
is aligned with the ultimate purpose of their existence and their core
value as human beings, they take it all a great deal more seriously.
Obviously, marriage is not the only instance. Nor do I mean to imply
that love demands that every marriage must continue. But we do well
always to be governed by the question: What does love require of me
in this situation?

3. Where the action in our life is, God is present and active.

Are you struggling with sexual addiction? That is the place
where you are encountering God and God is encountering you. Are

you working to overcome the damages of your childhood? That is the area where you and God are most engaged. Are you dueling with depression? There is nothing of greater significance in your relationship with God right now than this core struggle. God is always where the action in your life is.

Why is this? Because God has a stake in what you make of yourself, and the areas of your life that most absorb your attention are the areas of greatest consequence in that regard. That is where your energy is. That is where you are making choices that have important consequences. The question is: What is the opportunity God is offering you in this area where the action is? What is God trying to give you? What is God inviting you to?

I know a man who fought the alcoholic battle all his life. I know him well because he was my father. Over the decades I watched the struggle shape him. His failures were the root of his humility. They were also the source of his abundant compassion. His struggle taught him self-awareness and an exacting self-discipline. He learned to be a truth teller. His weakness threw him again and again on God, and carved out the channels of his spiritual life. His need for human support led to friendships that profoundly influenced his becoming, and in which he gave much to others of his love and acquired wisdom. Was his alcoholism a curse or a blessing? Hard to say. Whatever it may have been in itself, he and God certainly made a blessing out of it. This core lifelong struggle of his was the place where he and God were most vitally engaged.

We somehow cling to the idea that spirituality is what happens when we are in church or reading our Bible. It is *really* happening always, especially in the areas of life which most hold our attention at any given time. The way I usually get people thinking about this in therapy is by asking the question: Where do you think God is in all this? Whatever brought them in is where the action is for them right now, so that is where God is especially engaged with them, with important spiritual ramifications.

The need for a reexpansion of our spiritual consciousness is brought home in a story from the timeless wisdom tradition:

> Once upon a time there was a forest where the birds sang by day and the crickets by night. Trees flourished, flowers

bloomed, and all manner of creatures roamed in freedom. And all who entered there were led to Wonder and Worship, for they felt the presence of God.

Then the Age of Unconsciousness dawned, when it became possible for people to construct buildings a thousand feet high, and to destroy rivers and forests and mountains. And houses of worship were built from the wood of the forest and the rock of the mountain. Flowers were brought inside, water was placed in fonts, and bells replaced the sounds of Nature.

And God suddenly had a much smaller home.

4. *God does not send us pain and suffering, but works with us in them for good.*

I am fully aware as I say this that there seems to be as much disorder as order in this world of ours, and there is massive human suffering. It is an enigma, especially if one believes in a good and caring God. For all of us, life is always a struggle in one degree or another, as we have to do many things we do not wish to do and bear many things we do not wish to bear. Why life could not be a little easier is something we often puzzle over. Yet the English essayist G.K. Chesterton utters a truth when he says: "That life is a gift, infinitely valuable and infinitely valued, requires no further proof than to put a pistol to the head of a pessimist."

But it is suffering that brings people to therapy. And the point of the principle above is to state clearly where God stands with respect to our suffering. It is not God who willed or caused our sexual abuse as children. It is not God who "sends" us cancer or AIDS. It is not God who brought about our divorce, "took" our child, caused us to be lonely, or decided to make us poor. Otherwise God is part of the problem, not of the solution.

Where then is God with respect to these events that affect us so profoundly? First, God is at our side grieving with us in our pain. Second, God is working with us to bring forth all possible good from these evils we suffer. Third, God is calling all people of good will to change the conditions which produce these evils. Because it is what we human beings do to ourselves and to each other that produces almost all the evils we suffer.

God, as creator, stands at the source of the reality in which we live, and to that extent is responsible for everything. But God's decision was to make a world genuinely distinct from self, and so to create it free. This freedom exists in some measure even in the simplest agents on the ladder of being, and is particularly broad at the human level. Because there is genuine freedom in the created world, there is much that God cannot control, whether to prevent or to produce. An immense amount depends on free created agency, and it is from bad human choices that most of our pain and suffering come, whether in individual cases or in the larger socioeconomic systems which oppress so many.[2]

Let us consider the suffering and death of Jesus as a case in point. The symbol of the cross has so often been viewed as a sign that God's plan is pain and suffering, that God sends us travail as trial or punishment, that it might even be contrary to the divine purpose to resist it. But this line of thinking represents a failure to distinguish Jesus' whole thrust from the fate which befell him as a consequence. He poured his energies not into getting up on a cross, but into teaching people how to live and freeing them from what ailed them. That was his heart's love, his project, his driving purpose. It was also God's project and purpose, which is why Jesus was doing it. Jesus was killed out of human malice. This was humanity's doing, not God's. He was killed for the same reason Mahatma Gandhi and Martin Luther King were killed. They were all cut down, like many before them, because they sharply challenged the status quo and profoundly threatened those who were benefiting from it. God never willed any of these violent deaths, but rather willed the work these individuals were dedicated to on behalf of justice and life for all. God's purpose is always life, which God actively promotes. When thwarted by contrary human choice, God labors to draw life even out of evil and tragedy, as in the case of Jesus' death.[3]

So if the question is, "What should our response as Christians be to suffering in our own or others' lives?" the answer is that our first response should be to try to remove it, as Jesus did. In this we join our energies and purpose with God's own. It is only when we have done everything we can to overcome suffering that we should accept the unsolved remainder, placing our trust in God, who works with us to draw out of suffering all possible good. Again the example of Jesus is instructive. His labors to alleviate pain wherever he encountered it are plain in the gospels. What is not as obvious, but is there, is how he resisted the suffering which others tried to inflict on him. When a crowd wanted to push him over a precipice, he thwarted them, walking through their midst to safety (Lk 4:28–30). When his enemies were trying to arrest him, he evaded them by remaining outside the city in lonely places (Jn 11:53–4). When they came to arrest him in the garden, he protested (Mk 14:48). When he was slapped in the face during his trial, he protested again (Jn 18:23). In short, Jesus did not submit gracefully to abuse, as if he deserved it or as if it was some kind of gift from God. In the end he submitted to a violent and unjust death only because there was no longer anything he could do—unless he wanted to give up his whole life's work in exchange for peace. At that point, when he could no longer resist, he entrusted his cause to God. And God proved trustworthy.

In therapy, we deal with people who are suffering, and we suffer with them. We wish we could deliver them, and often find we cannot. We can only stand with them and, despite all our best professional efforts, mitigate but a portion of their pain. Yet we stay with the struggle, and encourage them in it. And all the while, in ways we cannot usually trace, even in our apparent defeat, God is effecting some transformation both of them and of ourselves. Putting our joint trust in this mystery at work in us is itself therapeutic. "For God is at work in you," as Paul says (Phil 2:13). Often clients need to hear such a word of faith from the therapist that their sufferings and struggles are meaningful.

5. The paradigm of death/resurrection is key to understanding our existence.

The death/resurrection of Jesus is the core around which Christian faith revolves. It is to Christians what the exodus is to Jews: the paradigm of hope in the midst of adversity. Just as Jews continually commemorate the exodus ritually to nurture their faith, so Christians continually commemorate the death/resurrection of Jesus in the eucharist to nourish theirs. In our daily experience, we are all too familiar with suffering and death. What we badly need is a reason to hope. The death/resurrection of Jesus gives us that reason, revealing to us that with God death is never the last word. Life is.

This principle has tremendous relevance to the therapeutic situation since it is suffering and the search for meaning and hope that bring people to therapy. The best hope available is the insight into God's workings given us in the climactic events of Jesus' life. These events are significant not just for Jesus personally, but constitute a paradigm or model with relevance for all of us. They reveal that God works within the tragedies of human existence to bring good out of evil, life out of death, meaning out of absurdity.

Everybody in therapy is either dying, or needs a push to die. When they are dying—for example, when they lose a loved one, are struggling in a relationship, or are revisiting the traumas of their childhood—they need to hear of resurrection from death, the good news that God is at work in them to bring them new life. When, on the other hand, they are afraid to die some death they must undergo, they need to hear about the death pole of the paradigm, death as the necessary path often to new life. The death in question might be finally letting go of a relationship that has proved to be a dead end, so that they can be open to another one. It might be taking the awful risk of letting someone know who they really are. It might be putting away their addictive substance and taking their first shaky steps without it. It might be surrendering manipulative efforts to get people to love them, choosing personal authenticity instead and taking their chances. It might be really leaving home and taking on the responsibilities of adult life. All of these decisions entail dying some death they have been afraid to die. The death/resurrection paradigm, which speaks to the spiritual dimension of this experience, is an enormous support.

I find "Holy Saturday" a useful metaphor for helping people interpret the shadowy time in which they sometimes find themselves between death and new life. "Holy Saturday" is that shapeless day between the Friday on which Jesus dies and the Sunday on which he is raised. In the annual reliving of these events in religious celebration, Holy Saturday is a kind of grey, vague, empty day on which nothing happens and one wonders what to feel or do. The acute pain of tragic death has abated somewhat, but nothing new yet stirs. In our lives, Holy Saturday sometimes lasts a while. But the death/resurrection paradigm reminds us that it is transitional nevertheless. Easter is coming.

6. God can and should be imaged in countless ways, no image being adequate to the mystery.

Both the Hebrew and Christian scriptures exhibit a rich variety of images in speaking of God. This truth is often lost on us, yet it has tremendous importance. Some of the biblical images are masculine, some feminine, some impersonal. God is king, military general, judge, lover. God is mother. God is fire, water, wind, bread. The Hindu pantheon has hundreds of thousands of "gods," but each is just an image for some aspect of the one overarching incomprehensible Mystery. There is a wonderful saying in Hinduism, perfectly consonant with Christian theology: "You are formless, O God, and your only form is our knowledge of you."

The Hebrew scriptures contain a divine commandment:

> "You shall not carve idols for yourselves in the shape of anything in the sky above or on the earth below or in the waters beneath the earth; you shall not bow down before them or worship them" (Ex 20:4–5).

The point of the injunction is to defend against the danger of confusing any mere image of God with the incomprehensible reality of God. And it applies as much to images in the imagination as to sculptures and paintings. The best protection against confusion is to have no image at all. "I am" is the only answer God gives Moses in reply to his question: "What is your name?" (Ex 3:13–14)

The problem with that is that we still feel a need to imagine God in some way in order to be able to relate, and we usually do imagine God in some way whether we realize it or not. We protect ourselves against idolatry when we rotate multiple images of God through our awareness and prayer. This helps us remember that each reflects but a facet of a mystery that goes beyond them all.

A theme in contemporary feminist writing is that we have impoverished ourselves by making an idol of Jesus' most used metaphor for God—Father—almost as if it were an exact depiction instead of a fruitful image. If we use no other metaphor, we talk ourselves into the idea that the image is the reality, that God really is masculine. One way the mistake has become genuinely harmful is that it is invoked as a justification for patriarchy in social arrangements, both inside and outside the church. Even short of that, the exclusive use of this particular metaphor impoverishes the prayer life of both women and men.[4]

Therapy may involve a reassessment of the client's dominant images for God. Persons who have suffered neglect or abuse at the hands of their human fathers may have great difficulty relating to God as Father. They need not. Women who have lived under patriarchy often suffer the inevitable second-class self-image which flows not only from their cultural conditioning, but also from the fact that the One at the top is masculine and his earthly incarnation, Jesus, is likewise male. It is easy to get brainwashed into the belief that women really *are* second-class. Large numbers of men and women alike have been catechized to image God mainly as Judge, so that the dominant emotion in their relationship with God is fear. For others, God is Taskmaster, the Great Perfectionist who will settle for nothing less in them. Living with this God is exhausting; it only deepens one's shame.

Major blockages to human growth can be cleared when people are helped to revise their images of God. Often, all that needs to be said when the therapist senses that an image is working against rather than for a person is essentially what this section says: "You know, that's only an *image* for God. It is not the reality. God is beyond our imagining. That is why the Bible uses so many different images for God—masculine, feminine, and impersonal—and warns us against making an idol of any of them."

The Christian mystic, Julian of Norwich, lived mainly with the image of God as Mother. Another eminent mystic, St. John of the Cross, evolved spiritually through many images, coming in the end to the image of God as "*nada*," or "nothing." His grapplings with God over time had purified away all the more graphic representations as inadequate to the mystery of his experience. In this book I use the image "Hidden Spring" to suggest how God is often experienced in the therapeutic process, as well as in our whole lives.

7. God often appears in human form.

All Christians celebrate the appearance of God in human form in Jesus of Nazareth. For many, that is where the idea of divine incarnation begins and ends. But that would mean that God is not usually present in the world, and has no other material expression than Jesus. As we saw earlier, the whole creation is charged with the grandeur of God. Everything is symbol and expression of the divine reality. As we move up the ladder of being toward human being, we have entities with increasing capacity to express the mystery of God. Karl Rahner was fond of insisting that *every* human being, not just Jesus, is a potential, and in some degree actual, self-revelation of God. In other words, what Jesus was most fully, each of us is called to be in the fullest possible measure. This is just an extrapolation of that foundational biblical notion that we are created "in the image and likeness of God" (Gn 1:26).

This principle means that we are always meeting God in the streets of the city. We meet God in one another. God is revealed to us in a special way in those persons who especially love us—friends, parents, children, spouses. That God loves us, and that we are valuable, is something we all believe—in a way. But we rarely feel it or really believe it until some human being incarnates that love for us, expresses it in human words and human touch. Then notional assent to the idea becomes *real* assent grounded in experience. Our friends, then, are true incarnations or sacraments—embodiments of the Invisible in the visible. For God often appears in human form.

This principle, in a particular application, lays bare the deepest reality of the therapist. The therapist is an incarnation of God, a key sacrament, in the life of the client. The therapist embodies and expresses God's care, interest, acceptance, hopes, challenge, and commitment in the life of the client. This does not mean that everything the therapist says flows from the mouth of God, for no human incarnation perfectly expresses God. It means that, in a general way, the therapist embodies the kinds of presence and activity that are God's own. It is a holy endeavor. For many whom life has handled roughly it is a saving relationship.

A healthy therapist, counselor, or spiritual director may shrink instinctively from so exalted a notion of the role. This is an appropriate humility and a necessary protection against confusing oneself with God. But surely God, the depth dimension of all reality, is present and active in the crucially formative relationship of therapy, and hence in the person of the therapist. How could God not be present when the relationship is essentially one of love?

> God is love, and the person who abides in love abides in God, and God in him or her (1 Jn 4:16).

> No one has ever seen God. Yet if we love one another, God dwells in us, and God's love is brought to perfection in us (1 Jn 4:12).

One way to conceptualize the therapeutic endeavor is to think of its main operations as either comforting or challenging the client. The therapist is always doing either the one or the other. And so is God, in dealing with any of us. The therapist accepts clients as they are, and where they are right now in the journey of their lives. This is a great gift. The therapist's office is a place of welcome, a setting where people can unburden themselves and find support, a haven where they can explore themselves in safety. The therapist is genuinely interested in how they are doing, wants the best for them, and is faithful in love through the progress and regress, the ups and downs of the period they spend together. The therapist affirms the client's goodness, confirms constructive choices, celebrates the victories, accepts the defeats without losing hope. All of this is comfort, and it nurtures life and development.

But if the therapist comforts, he or she also challenges, for this, too, is an office of love. The therapist confronts what the client is doing wrong, points out what the client is forgetting or failing to see, indicates poor choices and their consequences, challenges false beliefs, pushes the client to do what they prefer not to do. This, too, is the embodiment and expression of God's activity in the life of the client, for this too is love—the tougher side of genuine caring.

Comfort and challenge are the two creative, saving hands of God. Pick any passage of scripture, and in it you will hear the word of God doing either the one or the other—now giving comfort and assurance, now chiding and challenging to a change of heart. Watch any good parent, and you will see them doing now the one, now the other. This is not the mere imitation of God. It is the very incarnation of God, the embodiment of the Invisible in the visible.

Nor is it only the therapist who incarnates God in therapy. The client does also, bringing both comfort and challenge to the therapist. Clients, too, are good and beautiful people. They inspire us. They stretch us. And they labor and are heavily burdened. "Whatever you did for the least of my sisters and brothers, that you did for me" (Mt 25:40).

8. We are neither naturally good nor naturally evil, but immensely malleable and ultimately responsible for our own becoming.

The book of Genesis recounts the story of an early sinful choice made by a man and a woman in a garden, a choice from which multiple resulting alienations are depicted. The only problem with this very pregnant myth about human temptation and sin is that some Christian theology has extrapolated it into a doctrine of the total corruption of the human person, so that we supposedly have no capacity to choose the good or even to think correctly unless we are redeemed from this "fallen state" of "original sin" by Christ. It is difficult to reconcile a dogma of total corruption and helplessness with our actual experience, both of ourselves and of others.

As if in reaction to this extreme condemnation of human nature, others who have reflected on the human condition insist on the essential goodness of the person—unless someone corrupts him or her. This doctrine makes human evildoing an exception or aberration. That does not square with our experience of ourselves or others either.

The truth seems to lie somewhere in the middle, and the Bible shows a good sense of it as it tells the story of God's people from generation to generation. The characters in the story actually do much that is good, even exhibit heroism on occasion. At the same time they are wayward. They are tempted by the glamor of evil, wander from the path, even sink into corruption. But they recover from that, too. Jesus deals with people as if they have a free choice. He calls them to the good, his invitation enfolding a presumption that they can say yes. Many do. Others do not. They are all free.

In creating us, it seems, God creates not so much a person, as the raw materials of a person. Our creation continues from birth until death, under the influence of our environment, and in virtue of our own free choices. The environment contains shaping elements both constructive and destructive. Environment differs from environment in their proportions of good and evil. It is obviously much more difficult to bring wholeness out of cultures of poverty, racism, gender bias, abuse, or addiction. It is far easier where love, opportunity, and good example abound. Whatever our situation, as we develop we take increasing control of our development, with a growing power of choice over possible reactions to what our surroundings present. Each of our choices paves the way for the next, making a similar choice easier, a different kind of choice harder. Both our conditioning and the habits we establish do limit our freedom, but always we are free in some measure, and therefore responsible for our choices. Grace, too—the empowering gift of God's love—is always available to us.

Whatever our context, we seem to find ourselves ever in a field of conflicting forces: a current pulling us toward evil, and a current pulling us toward good. Around us stand models of both. If "original sin" means anything, it denotes the downward pull around us and, sympathetically, inside us. It is the history of human failure rolling down the generations with destructive effect. If "grace" means anything, it names the upward pull inside and around us—the call to conversion, the empowerment, the salve of healing, the surprise of liberation. Both forces are ever operative, and we do our self-creation within their tangled matrix.

The significance of this principle for therapy is manifold. It supplies a corrective for those weighed down with a conviction that they are evil at the core. At the same time, it offers a warning to those who have an exaggerated sense of their righteousness, unaware of their weakness and vulnerability to the lure of evil. Examples abound of how, placed in conducive circumstances, anyone of whatever previous standing somehow becomes an abuser, an embezzler, a betrayer, a murderer, a suicide. The principle reminds us of our plasticity, and of the responsibility we carry for our own becoming. "The devil made me do it" is no excuse. Neither can anyone say, "A person with my past hasn't got a chance." Always we have a choice. Sometimes the choice is to open ourselves to grace, or to get down on our knees and beg for it.

9. God's will for us is found within our own deepest wanting.

This is a principle for those who seek to do God's will in the important decisions of their lives—but sometimes wonder how to discern what God's will is. It indicates where to look. The principle has just one presupposition: that one's life is oriented to God, i.e., that one's fundamental intention in life is to live in harmony with God's values and purposes.

The principle as stated follows simply, but not always so obviously, from God's love for us. If God loves us, then God wants us to be ourselves, to have what is good, to do what expresses our true self and hence gives us satisfaction. The principle asserts the convergence between what we most deeply want and what God wants for us. Sometimes people think the two are opposed, as if God were against us rather than for us.

Is it God's will that I be a priest, or marry and have a family? That I stay with my marriage, or leave it? That I put my mother in a nursing home, or keep her at home?

First, God does not have a will for the details of my life. God leaves those to me. God has rather a general purpose for my life. As the prophet Micah puts it:

> This is what Yahweh asks of you, only this:
>> To live justly,
>> to love tenderly,
>> and to walk humbly with your God (Micah 6:8).

Micah here presents God's will very simply, in terms of three broad values. By contrast, many Christians conceive of God's will as a very detailed plan for their lives which it is very hard to bring to light. Yet both the Hebrew and Greek words in the Bible for God's will mean "God's yearning,"[5] a term much more suggestive of broad purpose than of specific detail. God presents us with a set of values according to which to order our lives, and leaves the particular decisions to us. There is no elaborate pre-plan. For this reason, the philosopher/

theologian Alfred North Whitehead thought it more accurate to speak of God's *purpose* rather than of God's will.[6] Seeking God's will, then, means aligning ourselves with God's purpose, and making our particular choices accordingly.

When faced with an important decision, people sometimes pray and then look for signs, or listen for God to speak some words to them. Well, it is good to pray, the better to align ourselves with God's purpose. But the place to look for the "signs" or "words" is deep within ourselves. When we have found what we most deeply want, we have found what we are looking for. God's purposes for us are planted deep within our being. God wants our true selfhood to unfold. In speaking here of our deepest wanting, I am obviously not talking about sudden impulse or passing whim, but about wanting that is persistent and flows from both emotion and reason.[7]

Carl Jung frequently urges this same basic idea, though speaking from a different conceptual framework. He stresses the importance of following our destiny, which flows out of our inner being. It is only in fidelity to this that we can find the meaning of our life and our true fulfillment. Jung urges listening carefully to our deepest self always— as it speaks in our nocturnal dreams, our daydreams, our visceral feelings of attraction or repulsion, consonance or dissonance—to keep finding our life direction. It is the same idea. The seeds of our destiny, or God's purpose for us, are planted deep within ourselves.

When in therapy, people seek help in finding God's will. This is the fundamental principle I offer. Presuming only that the orientation of your life is toward God, after looking at all sides of the matter in question, what do you most deeply want to do? That is what God wants you to do.

10. Good people are tempted by what seems morally or spiritually good.

It is plain that good people are *attracted* to what seems morally or spiritually good. But why do I say "tempted"? Because good people are sometimes destroyed by their own goodness.

This was one of the great discoveries of St. Ignatius Loyola. He detected a difference in the patterns of temptation he experienced at various points in his development. Then he observed the same phenomenon many times in other people whom he guided spiritually. Those whose lives are headed in a bad direction are tempted by gross evil. Those whose lives are oriented toward God do not find such prospects alluring, but are tempted instead by what seems morally or spiritually good.[8] For example, they think they should devote even more time to prayer than they already do, or be even more self-effacing, or impose an even stricter fast on themselves, or work even more hours in the service of others. If they are seduced by these apparent calls to a greater holiness, they are eventually destroyed by their own goodness, and that is why these attractions are temptations. Good people are very subject to them; they seem like promptings of the Holy Spirit. It requires the counsel of a spiritually experienced guide to help them differentiate the invitations of the Holy Spirit from these temptations. Unassisted, they easily fall prey to the perils entailed in their own goodness.

The key indicators for discerning which attractions are really from God are whether they produce true inner peace, and also whether in practice they produce the long-range good. Sometimes one has actually to try them to find out.

All of us sometimes need the help of a spiritually mature person in judging whether what we are doing or considering doing is really good. It is not only in matters of religious observance, but also in practical matters of daily life that we can be seduced by the specious good. We can easily be over-responsible for others, willing to be taken advantage of, unable to say no, or burdened in spirit by the suffering of the world. We think we *must* do what we do, or *must* suffer what we suffer; it seems to us a moral or spiritual imperative. We often need assistance in finding a truer sense both of our personal limitations and of what God is really asking.

****

These are the principles I use most in relating the spiritual to the therapeutic process. They are foundational faith convictions, and come up regularly in the therapeutic dialogue. They link particular concerns with more ultimate concerns. They often put matters in quite a different light, and so amount to a reframing. Often they are liberating. Sometimes they supply additional motivation. Always they highlight the presence and activity of God in the matters the client is grappling with, enabling the client to make a more conscious response to that.

In sum, the principles are these:

1. God wants life for us.
2. The purpose of our life is to learn how to love.
3. Where the action in our life is, God is present and active.
4. God does not send us pain and suffering, but works with us in them for good.
5. The paradigm of death/resurrection is key to understanding our existence.
6. God can and should be imaged in countless ways, no image being adequate to the mystery.
7. God often appears in human form.
8. We are neither naturally good nor naturally evil, but immensely malleable and ultimately responsible for our own becoming.
9. God's will for us is found within our own deepest wanting.
10. Good people are tempted by what seems morally or spiritually good.

Part Two

STORIES OF COUNSELING

About the Stories That Follow

The next six chapters apply the principles I have developed to therapeutic practice. These are stories of actual therapies I have done, written largely in the form of dialogues, with a sprinkling of personal reflections as the work unfolds. Though they are stories of actual therapy, let me be clear about what they are not.

First, they are not verbatims. A verbatim of a single therapy session would fill a chapter. But each of these therapies lasted at least a year, some of them several years. Trying to tell the story in a single chapter entails very judicious selection, and much compression even of what is chosen. The dialogues presented here are not verbatims even of the exchange the client and I had on the topic they cover. They simply try to capture the essence of it.

Second, I reconstruct these therapies to bring out a particular point—the spiritual dimension of our work. My purpose is to show where the spiritual springs into view and how the client and I work to integrate it into the therapeutic process. Because I am highlighting that, I cannot accurately convey the proportions of things. The spiritual dimension appears more prominently than it would were I able to recount the whole story of our time together.

Third, because in these accounts I sometimes develop a spiritual idea a little bit to make its import clear, it may sound as if I do much of the talking in sessions and teach theology at length. Actually, in matters spiritual, as in other matters therapeutic, my bent is to work collaboratively with the client toward the truth we seek. Again, it is considerations of space and the point I want to get across that give the stories their present form. It is a "literary form" which allows me to portray some things well, but at the sacrifice of some others.

All the accounts contain many disguises to protect the privacy of the clients and other persons involved. Each client has read their story and approved it for publication.

Everything I have said here applies also to the final case study, chapter 9, except that I am the client in that story, and it contains no disguises.

4.

The Man Who Hated Himself

Chuck, 35, came in to talk about his marriage. He was miserable. A shy man with tousled hair, dressed in plain shirt, jeans, and boots, he avoided eye-contact completely as he told his story. Some eight years before, while he was in the Navy, he had married a woman from Peru whom he had known for just two weeks.

"No one who had a choice would ever marry me," he explained. "There are a lot of reasons why I believe that, but I don't want to go into them now. My plan was to meet someone from a very poor country and bring her to the United States. I figured she would forever be grateful and would always love me on that basis. I didn't think I was capable of much of a relationship, but I figured a poor woman would be loyal to me, and we'd at least have a good sex life, which I wanted very much." He laughed, and I could see it was out of contempt for himself. He probably thought I held the same opinion.

"Well, it hasn't worked out at all. She's not grateful. We fight all the time. And there's no sex." He laughed again, embarrassed. "Another thing," he said. "I didn't know it at the time, but she had two children, each by a different man. We were in the States before she told me that. Naturally she wanted to bring them here; that was her plan from the outset. So, you see, each of us had a hidden agenda. Anyway, seeing it was the only decent thing to do, one by one I brought her children up here, which is immensely expensive and very troublesome besides, there's so much red tape. Then, three years ago we had a child of our own."

I was riveted to his narrative. What an incredible story. How low this man's self-esteem, that he believed only this kind of marriage was possible for him. How thoroughly whatever trust they started with must have been shattered when she told him about the children. And how the marital arrangement must have been shaken up again as each child was added. As Chuck filled in the picture, I learned that his wife now controlled everything, and he could get nowhere, either by trying to have a rational exchange or by taking a strong stand. As a Christian and an experienced family therapist, I believe in marital permanence as a general rule. But I am also convinced that God does not want us to drag out a miserable existence, or make others miserable, just to be "faithful." As a therapist, my general approach is to listen to people with care, and then give them my honest responses.

"What you are describing is not a marriage," I said. "I know you live together as a sort of family, and went through a church ceremony at the beginning. But whatever this arrangement might be called, it is not a marriage."

"I know," he said. "I talked to my pastor about it, and he said the same thing." Enlightened pastor, I thought. "I'm here because I heard you were a priest as well as a good marriage counselor, and I wanted to run it by you and see if you thought there was anything I could do."

"Well, I think you've got to start by talking to your wife. Tell her how unhappy you are. Tell her as far as you are concerned the marriage is on the line, and ask her what *she* wants to do. If she wants to save it, tell her what changes would be necessary for you to be interested. Find out what she's unhappy about. If she wants to come in to work on it with you, I'd be glad to help in whatever way I can." I believe the first tack when marital crisis occurs is to rise to the challenge and work to save the marriage if possible. Crisis time is growth time, and God is there as the spouses face the call to conversion. When one person is seriously considering divorce, it is only fair that the spouse be told the truth and given a chance to respond before it is too late.

Chuck agreed that was the thing to do, thanked me for the session, made another appointment, and sheepishly left. He returned alone two weeks later to say that his wife flatly refused to see any counselor. He had several times tried to engage her in looking at their issues. "Same old story," he said. "We can't talk. She shouted that if I wanted a divorce I could go get one, but I better not expect ever to see the kids again. Apparently the crazy life we live doesn't bother her that much. That's about as far as we got."

I suggested he wait a few days, and try again, and, if that failed, maybe another time later. It really did sound like an impossible situation, and Chuck's feeling of hopelessness was palpable. I said I didn't tell people what they should do, because only they fully knew the actual situation, and it was they who had to bear the consequences of whatever choices they made. He understood that. Plain though his appearance, he was obviously very intelligent.

"Can a Christian ever in good conscience seek a divorce?" he asked.

"I believe so," I said. "In some cases it seems to be the most loving thing to do, and love is always the norm."

"But what about those teachings of Christ in the Bible that forbid it?"

"Christ did articulate a very high ideal for Christian marriage, and it is always worth striving for. But not every couple can reach it. In fact, some marital situations are really awful. Then I think we have to ask whether God really wants us to live this out for the rest of our lives. Is it good for the people involved?"

"My situation certainly doesn't seem to be good for the people involved. There's no marriage. I'm miserable. The kids are living in a terrible environment. If we're not fighting, we're totally ignoring one another."

"In the end, it is always love that we try to be faithful to. Love is the highest Christian norm. It is higher than any particular norm, such as the ideal of marital permanence. And love always asks: What is good for everyone involved in this situation? What is the best decision I can make, taking everyone's welfare into account, including my own?"

"It's helpful just to talk about this and try to sort it out. I'll have to think about it some more."

"I don't know what you will choose or what you should choose, Chuck. But I believe that if you make your decision with care, God will accept it whatever it is. Wouldn't anyone who loves you?"

It was some months before Chuck contacted me again. When he came, he told me he had filed for divorce and moved out, while continuing to support the family. It had, of course, been an extremely difficult decision. But once he had made it, he felt the rightness of it. All the kids came regularly to see him, especially his own son. Then he said his wife was already seeing another man, which somehow really hurt in spite of how terrible their marriage had been. In fact, he told me, the man had moved in with the family within a month of Chuck's departure. With that he broke down and sobbed. I let him cry. How hard divorce is. This man had had so little love in his life, and now what seemed his best hope had ended in failure. More on his life story was about to come. For he had returned not to talk more about the marriage, but to do therapy on his own personal problems.

The Childhood in the Background

Chuck described a father who was unaffectionate and generally unavailable, and who had very little insight into himself. Not only did Chuck not feel loved; he felt his father positively disliked him and often said and did things to hurt him. But, Chuck said, his father would never acknowledge something like that, even to himself. Chuck's relationship with his father was very important to him, and it was himself he blamed for its failure. He felt fundamentally flawed.

Chuck described his mother as domineering and needy. Unable to get the love she wanted from her husband, she drew Chuck close and tried to get it from him. Chuck carried a lot of guilt from this relationship, which, although it was not explicitly sexual, had plenty of emotional/sexual confusion in it. It was still not clear to him whether his mother really loved him, or only used him to meet her own needs. He came out of his childhood very poorly equipped for life—unclear about his selfhood, uncertain of his manhood, totally lacking self-confidence, at a loss how to relate. He realized he needed to get away from his family, so he went away to college, trying to put as much distance as possible between himself and them. But feeling as bad about himself as he did, he holed up in his room except for classes, and eventually had a breakdown severe enough to require hospitalization. That, of course, damaged his self-esteem even further.

Years had gone by now, and by dint of some helpful therapy after his psychic breakdown and a lot of subsequent reading in psychology, Chuck had gained much insight into himself and his problems. But somehow the bad feelings were all still solidly in place. That's the trouble with insight: it doesn't often change feelings or behavior very much. A new and different *experience* seems to be required for that. "I hate myself," Chuck said with his little laugh. "Always have."

That is what most concerned me. That was the core issue for therapy, and all my experience told me it is a tough one. What could I do for Chuck?

Well, first of all, I could care for him. And the good news was that that would be easy: I genuinely liked him. I found him so real, so honest, and so full of integrity. My affection and concern would supply something of what had been so lacking in his childhood. Then I took stock of all he had going for him, that on which I could build. He was intelligent and articulate. He had two long-standing, close friendships. He held a good job. I would reflect all of his achievements and his personal assets back to him. I would labor also to reduce the negativity in his consciousness. I would call attention to his self-putdowns, and ask him to stop doing that. I would call attention to his avoiding eye-contact, and ask him to take the risk of seeing and being seen. I would encourage him to assess his parents critically, and put some of the blame there rather than all on himself and his defects. I would get genuinely interested in his life, and walk with him wherever he led me, sharing with him my honest reactions. I would accept all of it, express empathy where I saw him suffering, affirm all I saw him do well, challenge assumptions and interpretations which seemed unwarranted and harmful. In short, I would relate to him over time as a caring human being. That would be the new and different experience that would bring Chuck some measure of healing. And as he became surer and stronger, I would nudge him toward forming other relationships. Ultimately, it is relationships that heal.

But I keenly felt the need of enlisting spiritual resources for this difficult therapy. In trying to help Chuck change his self-hate to self-love, I would call attention again and again to the spiritual dimension, encouraging him to relate to it with fuller awareness and openness. Both of us needed it.

And so, one day when he was sunk in self-deprecation, I said: "Chuck, your parents didn't love you very well. But there is One who has always loved you. God takes delight in you, and God's love is your ultimate validation. Parents are relative. God's love in your life is solid as a rock."

"I do believe in God's love," he said sincerely. "But it's pretty abstract most of the time."

"It is," I said. "I'm not talking mainly about a feeling, but about a conviction firmly held and strengthened over time by prayer. You know, there are a lot of people who were not loved very well by their parents. But God seems to send others along the way who do love them and fill in what was missing at the beginning—grandparents or other relatives, teachers, friends. Look at your own life. You've talked about two people who have been good friends to you for years. They see you more clearly than your parents were able to, and they love you. They are not only God's gifts; they actually incarnate God's own love for you. They make it concrete and palpable."

"I've never looked at it that way," he said. "I've never connected the two. Both Bob and Jim really have loved me. And they know a lot about me." He was silent awhile as he pondered God's involvement in these two friendships.

Psychic Breakdown

Not long after that, Chuck told me more about his two psychic break-downs. Both of them were signs to him of how "screwed up" he was. To me they were signs that he had been holding in things he needed to feel, express, and share. They were dramatic calls to a change in his way of being. Also, the way Chuck handled them told me of his integrity, courage, and desire to grow. The first episode had occurred during his first year of college, the second shortly after he graduated and was working. The first time he was hospitalized and heavily med-icated. He left the hospital patched back together again, but without having faced any of his issues. When the second break came, he decided not to seek help, because he did not want medication to drown out awareness. He had read a lot of psychology in the interval, and he knew that his task was to let the contents of his unconscious come to consciousness so that he could process them. Because he had done this all on his own, he wanted to open it up to me. It was with trepidation that he did so.[1]

"A lot of sexual stuff came up," he began. "Several times I had visions of myself sucking my father's penis." He was obviously embarrassed. "I was terrified it meant I was homosexual, or that I somehow wanted to seduce my own father. What kind of horrible per-son was I? You know that I actually had almost no relationship with my father. I always had the feeling that he hated me. I still do. The few times he actually did anything with me as a child, it seemed he wanted to shame me. When I was five or six, he took me out to play catch, and I got hit in the face with the ball three times. Each time he asked me, 'Well, do you want to stop now?' I think he truly wanted me to. It really seemed he wanted to hurt me and make me give up. After that day, we never played again. Around that same time he took me out to teach me how to ride a bike. It was the same thing. Twice I fell, and the second time was the end of the lesson. He kind of smiled as if to say what a hopeless case I was, and went back in the house. We never talked about it. As far as learning how to ride a bike or play baseball were concerned, I was on my own. If these had been isolated incidents, they probably would not have had any lasting impact. But I'm just trying to give you a few examples of how the relationship was always, which is why it cut so deep. To give another example, it was the same with learning to drive a car when I was sixteen. He never offered to teach me. I never asked. He gave me no sexual information or advice either, and I've always struggled with my sexuality and what it means to be a man."

I shared my incredulity and pain as I heard these childhood experiences, especially the early ones. I wanted to validate Chuck's sense that he had been wronged. As I listened, I was envisioning the impact particularly of the early incidents on the young child. The child cannot stand back from his father and say to himself, "I see that my father has very little capacity to love." He draws the more obvious (a child's) conclusion: "I am inadequate. I am unlovable. There is something fundamentally wrong with me." This feeling, for it is a feeling more than a thought, was still dominant in Chuck's relationship to himself and everyone else. He hated himself, and felt rejection was exactly what he deserved. Such a conviction determines one's whole stance in life. To overturn it, another authority has to speak strongly and repeatedly to the contrary. Even then, eradication is difficult, so devastating is the original sentence. So as part of my work with Chuck I kept chipping away at that core conviction whenever it showed. For me, the ultimate validation of a person's worth and goodness is God's creation and love of that person. I try to embody that love as a therapist.

"Chuck," I said. "Let's go back to those sexual images you described. I think they are important. Were there any others?"

"Yes. But the other recurrent image was just as bad as the one I told you about," Chuck said. "It was of me as an adult nursing at a mother's breast. It came many times. I must be really fucked up."

"This will probably sound strange to you, Chuck, but I see these images very differently. Let's put them in context. Consider your childhood. You were desperate for love. You never got it from either parent, yet you continued, naturally, to hunger and thirst for it. Now sex is basically about love. That is why it has such power over all of us. It is love we long for, closeness and comfort with someone. That is what I think sucking on your father's penis means. It is as if you are saying to your father, 'Can I get you to notice me? Can I get you to feel something for me? Can I draw some life from you, some manhood, whatever it is I need to make me feel all right about myself?' I don't think the image has anything to do with homosexuality or seduction."

Chuck was looking at me intently, surprised and moved by what I was saying.

"I think it's the same thing with the maternal image. It's not about incest or even about sex. It's about love. What better symbol of love than a mother's breast? What does an infant most need from his mother? A safe place and nourishment. You didn't get that. You longed for it. As an adult you've continued to hunger for it. The unconscious speaks to us symbolically of what is stirring deep within. Your unconscious tells you of your profound yearning for love, and for connection with your parents in particular."

Chuck was crying now. A huge load of anxiety had been lifted, and in its place a naming of what dwelt so powerfully in his soul. He recognized it and was feeling it. But I was reflecting simultaneously in another plane, and wanted to add something.

"There is an even deeper level of meaning here, Chuck. Both the penis and the breast are symbols of God in many of the religious traditions of the world. And the reason is fairly obvious. Both penis and breast have to do with the giving of life and the expression of love. And both are filled with wonder and mystery. Those are the very things that God is—giver of life, lover, wonder and mystery. The fact that phallus and breast are charged with divinity for us helps account for the powerful sway sex exercises over us, a potency that cannot be fully accounted for merely by the sense pleasure sex gives. At bottom, Chuck, it is God you long for, God you reach for, and God you actually encounter in the images you have shared."

As we talked all this over, I added something else. "I don't know if you know the writings of Carl Jung, but he is one of the giants in the mapping of our psychic life. In his autobiography he recounts one of his earliest religious experiences. While still a child he had a vision of a temple in which a gigantic phallus was enshrined. It astonished him. At first he thought he blasphemed even to entertain such an image. Over time he learned that both phallus and breast have long been symbols for the male and female aspects of God in the religions of the world.[2] Chuck, I think the churches have done us a tremendous disservice by driving such a wedge between sexuality and divinity, as if the two were opposite poles, almost like good and evil. Sexuality is actually suffused with the sacred. It is profoundly numinous."

This conversation prompted Chuck, with his strong intellectual bent, to spend more time with Jung, whom he knew only slightly. What had at first sounded fantastic proved on investigation to be solidly grounded, and the reading extended and deepened our therapeutic work on Chuck's sense of his sexuality.

Operative Images of God

"I have to tell you about something I always do to myself that I wish I could change," Chuck said one day. "If I have a good time—even if there is no question of its being a sin or anything like that—I automatically punish myself. Pleasure has to be paid for, I figure." He laughed his self-deprecating laugh. "I don't deserve anything good, see? So if by some chance I do get feeling good, I know that some terrible evil will surely follow to put it right. So I anticipate it by inflicting some pain on myself, to stave off the punishment. It all goes back to when I was a little kid. When I said something bad, my mother would wash out my mouth with soap. So I got to beating her to the punch. I would go and wash out my own mouth with soap and come and show it to her, so she wouldn't have to do it. I preferred doing it to myself."

Again I felt sad as I heard this new variation on an old theme. It was so patent how thoroughly Chuck had learned to hate himself, and how he had projected onto God his early experiences of mom and dad. He could not conceive of anyone loving him or really wanting his good. His childhood experience had persuaded him that it was not good and happiness that were natural and normal, but evil and suffering. Goodness was a fluke, and he certainly had no right to it even when it chanced to appear.

"Your God is awfully small, Chuck," I said. "So stingy. So vindictive. So cruel. You really give God a bum rap."

"I guess I do," he said. "In my head, I don't really believe it. But if you ask what I live out of, I have to admit I live out of that kind of image of God. I don't feel safe at all. I'm a tremendously anxious person. If I touch something, I worry I'm going to get a disease. If I get a promotion at work, I worry it is a setup for soon getting fired. At times since I started this therapy with you, I really feel pretty good. Immediately I'm terrified. That's not for me, and I better get rid of it quick. So I inflict some pain on myself to feel bad again so I can be safe."

I realized that this was not a conceptual, but an experiential matter. His intellect knew what was true, but his emotional life had been stamped by a different experience. That early conditioning would have to be countered by something that could touch the imagination and emotions, not just the mind.

"Chuck, have you ever had an experience of being loved by God?"

"Yes, I have. It was quite a few years ago. I was experimenting with mushrooms as a psychedelic. A couple of times when I was in an altered state of consciousness, I felt really loved by God. It was absolutely wonderful. I felt very close to God."

To me, mushrooms or no mushrooms, that experience is real. Countless people have had it. It does not depend on a drug.

"I'm so glad to hear that. That experience can be trusted. The question is, how could you make it more operative in your life? I mean, how could you renew or deepen or draw upon it more, so that you could live from it instead of from this crazy notion of God that comes right from your parents?"

"I see where you're going. The answer is, it's not easy. I went to a workshop on centering prayer, and found that it doesn't work for me. Some people can just sit quiet for a few minutes and find their center. There's no way I can do that; I have way too many layers of shit to get through. It takes an hour or more to get through them to that deep down center, if I can get there at all. Recently though, I found a way to do it. I made a Progoff Journal Workshop. He teaches a method for ploughing through all those layers of shit and reaching that core. It takes quite awhile for me, but it has worked a couple of times."

"That sounds perfect. Would you start doing that on a regular basis? I think you really need to get back to that deep down place in yourself where God lives. And it will take regular meditation to do it."

"I'll try it this week. I just have to set aside the time."

"Great. One other thing, Chuck, and this requires some courage. Take your chances with God more. God really wants life for you, fullness of life. God's love means that, or it means nothing. So if you enjoy something, just give thanks. Resist the urge to impose pain on yourself to pay for it. Just let come what comes. And tell me if anything bad happens as a result, OK?"

"Sounds scary, but I'll give it a try."

When he came the next time, he told me he had used the Progoff method of meditation, and had been able to reach that place inside where he felt safe, good, and loved. I was delighted, and encouraged him to keep doing it. The transformation of worldview which we were seeking would take time.

The Late Stages of Therapy

As our work continued beyond that first year, Chuck used our sessions to discuss many things going on in his life. He continued to support his family, and to spend a lot of time with his little son. He saw the other kids regularly too, and was encouraged to note that they actively sought to continue their relationships with him. When we talked, Chuck looked me in the eye more, and laughed at himself less. Though he continued to live with considerable anxiety about terrible things that might befall him, he told me his fear was gradually growing smaller. He continued to be supported by his close friends, and enjoyed a growing sense of being appreciated at work, not just for what he did but for who he was. Again he received a promotion.

We talked about what it means to be a man. He recounted how he had thought it involved passing a number of tests—of a certain physical strength and endurance, of military service, of successful marriage, of fatherhood. He did not think he had made it, though he did not know exactly what he still needed to prove. I told him I knew and respected as men many individuals who had never passed those particular tests, yet were mature and admirable men. I suggested he think not so much in terms of what it means to be a man, as what it means to be a full human being. I said I thought Jesus of Nazareth was the best exemplification of that I had encountered, though the gospels tell us nothing of his physical strength, military service, or marriage. Mature personhood consists of a set of moral qualities we instinctively admire in women and men, and the attainment of "machismo" has very little to do with it.

Chuck started putting more energy into trying to meet a woman who might be a companion to him. I regarded it as a good sign of the healing that gradually deepened. He was drawn at first to topless bars, where for a price you can meet anyone you wish. But as he followed up by phone on a couple of those encounters, he discovered that the women were not particularly mature or reliable. They were more wounded than he. He began to seek in more promising places, where people were engaged in the kinds of activities he enjoyed. A marriage is essentially a friendship, not a sexual liaison (though sex is a wonderful part of it), and a friendship lives on shared interests, values, and activities. Chuck could not long be happy with a woman who did not share at least some of his rich spiritual and intellectual life and want to help him raise his child.

More than once in these later stages of therapy Chuck remarked, "I feel very grateful to be alive. I am thankful for everything that has happened to me and everything I've done. It is a privilege just to experience life. It might never have been. All of it is sheer gift. So I try to live each day fully." What a grace, I thought. Chuck's life had not been an easy one. Yet he had come to this remarkable attitude. Surely that was God's doing.

When I asked him if he would mind my writing up his story for a book I was writing on the spiritual dimension of therapy, he responded enthusiastically. "If my life could be of any use to anyone else, that would mean a lot to me. It would make it all worthwhile—I mean, even more worthwhile. What a great opportunity. Thank you."

5.

Battling Depression

Cathy was depressed. She came in with her husband, because she feared this latest in a series of depressions might sound the death knell to their marriage. But as the three of us talked, it became clear that the marriage was solid, a covenant of some 28 years that had nurtured three children, two of them adopted. Cathy's husband had weathered her depressive episodes many times, and had learned patience. It was hard for him, but it was harder for Cathy, naturally, and it was with her that I elected to work. A woman of 50 or so, Cathy was attractive, refined, and engaging. But she carried a lot of pain, and the tears came easily.

"I feel like a complete failure as a mother. The kids aren't doing well at all. Our oldest son is gay. Our older daughter is a recovering alcoholic. And our younger daughter is alcoholic, too, but I'm not sure she's recovering. We had to tell her recently that she couldn't live at home anymore, because she wouldn't give up her drinking." And the tears really flowed now.

It is always amazing to me how quickly some people trust. This woman did not know me at all, and she was laying out her heart. What a sacred trust. Not that she had anything to fear; I felt anything but judgment. We do not make our children alcoholic or gay. We may pass along a genetic predisposition to alcoholism (or depression, for that matter), which we very possibly inherited ourselves. But we can hardly take responsibility for that. Homosexuality seems to be congenitally determined rather than to be based on how one is raised. Cathy was faulting her parenting for things beyond her control. Good parenting is mainly a matter of giving children the love and attention they need, and then providing them with good opportunities and common sense guidance. As I came to know this couple, I felt sure they had done that. With the kids in their twenties and gone from home, Cathy's parenting was done and the house was empty. I wondered whether a good part of Cathy's depression was rooted right there.

Transitions

Depression is still more of a mystery to the mental health field than that field would like. It varies greatly from person to person, and seems usually to have multiple causal factors. I find it helpful to think of three factors in particular: our circumstances, the way we think about our circumstances, and our biochemistry. Often, more than one of these elements are implicated. My first reading of Cathy was that she was in a life transition, and she had to let go of her children and find a new reason to live. I would keep an ear tuned to her thinking and the signs of depressive biochemistry.

"As you may know, Cathy, I don't have children, but I have an older sister who has raised nine of them in two different marriages. And she remarked to me one day that after raising six or so she had discovered something: 'I've learned that when they reach 18, my work of parenting is over. They may not be fully mature; they may even be still at home for a time. But they neither seek nor listen to any more parenting from us. We've given them what we have to give. We hope it's planted. Whatever they still need, they'll have to get someplace else. So I let go and just let that happen. It has made it a lot easier.' "

Cathy smiled. "I think what she says makes sense. My kids are well past 18—but I'm still trying to mold them. It's just so hard to see them flounder. That's when I step in."

"What do you think your kids really need from you now?"

She thought a moment. "Oh, they need a lot of things." She laughed. "But what do they need from me? I know they still need love. And encouragement." There she ran out.

"I think that's exactly right. They need love and encouragement. They want the two of you to be their friends. I bet they'd value that immensely. But your advice?" I paused. "Did you want your parents' advice after you left home?"

She laughed.

"But, Cathy, if your parenting days are over, what are you going to do with the rest of your life? You've been a parent for 25 years. If that's gone, what are you going to fill the vacuum with? You have to create a new identity for yourself and a new meaning for your life. Otherwise, how could you not be depressed?"

"I do feel empty. I guess that's why I keep turning to the kids. A new identity? I see what you're getting at, but my mind just goes blank."

So we talked about new possibilities—classes, part-time job, volunteer work, hobbies, her relationship with her husband. Besides activities that would give her life new meaning, I added the need for regular exercise to help keep depression at bay. And then, knowing that Cathy took her Christian life very seriously, I wanted to put all the issues in a spiritual perspective.

"Cathy, I know that you take your faith life seriously. What do you think your spirituality has to do with what we've talked about so far?"

She thought a minute. "I'm glad you asked that. I have to think about it." She was silent. "I know God is with me in all this, helping me."

"Yes. And what do you think God might be calling you to at this time in your life?"

"I guess maybe it would be trust. It seems I'm at a turning point, and I can't see the future. All I know is that it's going to be different. So I have to trust God to lead me, and open new doors for me, and help me do what I'm supposed to do."

"That really sounds right. Anything else?"

"Taking off from what your sister said, I see I have to let go of the kids. I can't take care of them anymore. I'll have to hand them over to God and the world, and hope that somehow they will get what they need. That's going to take an immense amount of trust on my part. But I know they don't want me hovering around them or worrying about them. They've told me that."

"That sounds right too. Anything else?"

"I can't think of anything else."

"Well, that's a lot. One additional thought I have is that I'm sure God doesn't want you to be depressed. Your life is God's gift to you, a thing to be enjoyed. So God supports you in your struggle to throw off this depression. I only mention this because sometimes people think God sends them things like this, and they're supposed to accept them. No, you will grow by struggling against your depression, not by accepting it."

"I like the sound of that. I do want to do God's will, even if it means accepting my depression. I do want to grow. But the way you're putting the two together sounds much more hopeful."

The Question of Medication

For six months, I didn't see Cathy. Then she came back.

"I'm depressed again," she said embarrassed. "It got a lot better after our sessions last time. I have let go of the kids. And I got a part-time job helping with the feed-in our church sponsors for street people. It's been just a wonderful opportunity for me. I'm learning a lot. And I love the people—most of them, anyway. My husband and I have been getting along great. But now in the last few weeks, I'm feeling down again, and I don't know why." Again the tears came. "I wake up in the morning and don't feel like getting up at all. I've got a terrible knot in my stomach. I drag myself through the day. Everything feels so difficult."

As we talked further, I noted that her life on the whole sounded very good. Yet somehow there was this heaviness. I could feel it in the room. It was evident in her whole demeanor.

Now I was thinking biochemistry as a contributing factor in her depression. She had made changes and had felt better for quite some time. There was no recent misfortune to explain her being cast down anew. Add to that the fact that depression had been recurrent in her life for some years, coming and going without nameable cause. We went over that history again, and then over the onset and circumstances of the current episode. Everything she said suggested that her biochemistry was involved. I suggested she see a psychiatrist for an evaluation, which might lead to medication. I collaborate on cases like this with a psychiatrist. He does his own evaluation, and decides whether or not to prescribe medication. I don't want automatic medication; I want a second opinion. In Cathy's case, the psychiatrist's decision was to put her on medication, and she showed a good response to it.

Medication is rarely a total answer. It is certainly not a substitute for facing one's life issues and working them through to some kind of resolution, growing through the process. Its purpose is not to put someone in a fog so they do not have to think, but only to put some kind of flooring under their emotional life so they *can* think clearly to work on their problems.

Medication is a spiritual issue in a certain sense. There are some Christians who believe faith is the answer to everything, and that prayer substitutes for medical interventions. While I believe in prayer, I also believe God leaves a great deal of responsibility to us, both in our personal lives and in the way we manage the world. God expects us to do everything in our power. In the present context, that entails using the best resources that both psychology and medicine have to offer. In my view, God works within, not alongside, ordinary means. I see, not a secular reality in which God occasionally intervenes, but a created reality permeated with divine activity.

While the medication was doing its work, Cathy and I continued ours. She asked more about the causes of homosexuality, and about the moral issues involved. As a follow-up to our discussion I suggested she read *The Church and the Homosexual* and *Taking a Chance on God* by John McNeill, a priest psychotherapist with much wisdom to offer in this area.[1] Cathy also shared the pain of watching her daughters' battles with alcoholism. I was happy to learn that she and her husband were already regular attendees at Alanon meetings, and had read a good bit on alcoholism.

Another problem she mentioned was dealing with the anger she sometimes felt in relationships. My ears perked up, because anger is often a factor in depression, and women particularly are conditioned to swallow their anger and be "nice." We worked on developing Cathy's assertiveness, because when she held her anger in, she ended by blaming herself for everything that was wrong, and became depressed. Cathy was a "good Christian" too, and she thought she was not supposed to get angry. This is a point on which spirituality has often been unhelpful. Actually, anger is a legitimate and useful human emotion, built into us by the creator for our protection. We need our anger. There is nothing wrong with feeling it; it is, in fact, useful information. The only moral issue is what we do with it. Sharing it in a constructive way when someone's behavior is bothering us is an appropriate act of self-love, and often an act of love for the other as well.

Another thing we worked on as part of the healing of Cathy's depression were the patterns of her thinking. We can make ourselves miserable in many ways: for example, by focusing on our deficits, by generalizing from a single failure, by catastrophizing from a small unfavorable indication, by blaming ourselves too much when something goes wrong, by expecting perfection of ourselves or others. A fine resource here is David Burns' *Feeling Good*, a popularization of the pioneering work in cognitive therapy by Aaron Beck.[2] Something that Cathy personalized, for example, was her children's infrequent calls and visits, which she interpreted to mean that she had failed as a mother. To me their pattern seemed quite normal and I said so. They were taken up with their own lives.

Visualization for Healing

I believe in the healing power of the imagination, and often use imaginative exercises such as focusing or guided visualization.[3] The imagination and emotions are closely linked. Cathy had spoken several times of a knot she felt in her stomach when she felt depressed, and one day I suggested we focus on that knot, because physical sensations often contain important emotions which need unpacking. I had her close her eyes and relax. Then I asked her to focus her attention on that knot, experience exactly what it felt like, imagine what it looked like, and invite it to speak about itself.

"It seems to be a fear of letting go," she said after a few moments. "It's a tightness, a holding." She was quiet. "Now I'm seeing my inner child. It has to do with her. She is afraid just to be. She feels as if she always has to do everything just right." Her imagination was getting these memories and doing these linkages all on its own.

"See if you can encourage her to do whatever she feels like."

Cathy said nothing for awhile. I let that be. Then I asked, "What's happening now?"

"I took her in my arms and embraced her. I told her she is all right just as she is, and doesn't have to be afraid of doing something wrong. I smiled at her and let her go, and now I am watching as she runs and skips." Pause. "Now she's jumping rope." Pause. "Now she's dancing." And Cathy was smiling with her eyes closed.

I was delighted with what was happening. It was exactly what she needed. "Great," I said. "Just watch her awhile, and keep encouraging her. Enjoy her." And I let several minutes pass in silence.

I see such inner experiences as graced. I do not produce them. Neither does the client, who feels they are given and is often completely surprised by what happens. When I see healing or liberation taking place, I see God at work, and I simply allow and support the person's savoring the experience as deeply as possible in the imagination and feelings.

In another session, Cathy complained of a nagging sense that there was something she was doing wrong which was the root of all her trouble, but she could not figure out what it was. She had expressed this sense on two previous occasions, but nothing had emerged over the months, and our combing had been thorough. In situations like this, I sometimes suggest a visualization in which the person takes his or her question or concern directly to Jesus. So I had Cathy close her eyes and I took her through some exercises to deepen her relaxation so that she could be completely focused.

"Now, Cathy, I want you to go in your imagination to some place that is pleasant and comfortable for you, and take a few minutes just to be there, noticing the sights and sounds and smells of the place." I left a little time. "Now ask Jesus to come to you there." Pause. "Take a minute really to see him and to notice how he joins with you." Pause. "Now tell him your concern." And I let some minutes pass, presuming they were dialoguing. Then I said, as I often do just to check for any trouble, "Tell me what's happening now."

"We're walking on the beach. I ask him what it is that I'm not seeing. He gives me no answer." She was silent. I decided just to let it keep unfolding. This takes some trust. "Now I hear a voice that says: 'Let go.'" And then Cathy began praying out loud: "Dear God, I give you Bill (her husband). I give you the kids. I give you all my fear." She was crying now.

I had already learned from Cathy that letting go—not worrying so much or trying to control everything—was the key to her peace, and so I wanted what was happening to deepen. "Cathy, see if you can conceive an image of letting go, any image at all." She was silent. "Tell me what's happening now."

"I'm soaring. I'm flying free."

"Notice what that feels like."

"It feels wonderful."

"Enjoy it awhile."

Cathy looked very peaceful. Then her expression changed. "I'm falling!" Good grief, I thought. What do I do now? I decided to do what I usually do in such situations, let the film keep rolling, hoping for the best. "I'm in a heap on the ground," she said dismayed.

"Just stay with it, Cathy. Let it continue to unfold." I waited a bit. "What's happening now?"

"I hear a voice that says, 'Try again.' " Silence. I waited. "I'm soaring again." She was smiling.

What a graced experience. Cathy would surely fall from time to time. Who doesn't? But she had just learned that she could get up and fly again. A few minutes later she told me she had made a soft landing. "Jesus is no longer here. And now I hear a voice that says, 'Trust. Trust.' "

I thought it a good place to stop. "Now take a minute to bring this to a close." She did, and opened her eyes.

I was remembering what we had started with—her sense that she was doing something wrong which she couldn't identify—and I had a sudden thought.

"Cathy, what do you make of the fact that Jesus had no answer for you when you asked what it was you were not seeing?"

"Hmm. That's interesting, isn't it? He didn't show me anything." She paused. "Maybe he was answering indirectly when he said, 'Let go,' and later, 'Trust.' Maybe that is what I am doing wrong—trying too hard."

"That has a ring of truth. It may be the answer you were looking for."

Accepting the Unsolved Remainder

Cathy was feeling good again, and asked to come every two months, just to maintain. She continued to take medication. For six or eight months she had a very positive report each time she came. It was wonderful to see her energy and her zest for living. Then another depression came. I have learned with depression-prone people on medication that when they are generally doing well on it but then suddenly start to sink without circumstantial cause, it often helps to make a change in the medication, increasing or decreasing the dosage, or trying another medication or combination. So I suggested she contact

her psychiatrist and tell her what was happening. But it also seemed
to me at this point that Cathy might possibly have to live with depressive episodes the rest of her life—though hopefully less lengthy and
less severe.

"Cathy, you've done an immense amount of work on your
depression. You've made significant changes in the way you live.
You've examined your thinking, and are working to eliminate negative patterns. You've taken medication, and it has helped. You've
worked on your spiritual life, and grown in the direction of letting go
and trusting God. You have struggled courageously with your depression, overcome a lot of it, and grown through the process."

"Yes, that's all true, and I was even starting to feel good about it.
But here I am again, right back where I started."

"Yes, that pains me too. I don't think of you as being back where
you started, but it is another down time. And I'm aware that as we
look back over your life, we see a cycle of these depressive episodes
stretching over many years. I hate to say this, but I am beginning to
wonder if perhaps these times are something you are just going to
have to live with."

"That sounds awful to me." Her voice quavered. "But part of me
thinks you might be right."

"I don't know if I'm right. I hope I'm not. But it is a possibility
you might have to prepare for. There's a wonderful line in Anthony de
Mello's book *Awareness*,[4] which I was reading again a couple of
weeks ago on my retreat. I found the whole book very helpful. I think
he is one of the genuinely enlightened ones of our day. Anyway, the
line goes something like this: 'Before I was enlightened, I was
depressed. Now I'm enlightened. I'm still depressed. But it doesn't
bother me so much anymore.' " Cathy laughed. We both did. "I think
that might be the goal for you too—to live with your depression when
it comes, but not let it bother you so much anymore. What de Mello
suggests is simply not to identify with it. Instead of saying, 'I am
depressed,' you say to yourself, 'There is depression there now.' The
'I' stays clear of it. It simply observes."

Cathy was silent, mulling this. "I know I do identify with it, and
then blame myself for it besides. I get swept up into it entirely.
Whether I could stand back from it or not, I don't know. I could try."
She paused. "But you know, Tom, I just wish I could see some *pur-*

pose in all this. I've prayed and prayed, but I just don't see any purpose in it at all."

"I couldn't tell you what the purpose is, Cathy. As you know, I don't believe God sends us our sufferings, so it doesn't have a purpose in that sense. But I do believe that God always works with us to bring good out of our misfortunes. Exactly how your depression has worked in your life, I cannot say. But I do know that you are a beautiful person today—deep, caring, spiritual. And this struggle has run right through the center of your life, so I suspect it has been a key factor in what you and God have created together."

"Thank you for saying that. It's something I can't see. It helps to hear it."

Destroyed by One's Own Goodness

In our next session, I came back to Cathy's blaming herself for getting depressed and frantically searching for what she was doing wrong. "There's one other thing I want to go over before we quit today. I notice that when you get depressed, you really do a job on yourself. You tell yourself you're a terrible wife and an awful person, and you believe again that there is something you're doing wrong that you've never identified, and in the end you have no peace at all, but just endless turmoil."

"That pretty well says it."

"If we look at that in spiritual perspective, it's a temptation."

"What do you mean, a temptation? I don't see that it is about sin."

"One of the great spiritual discoveries of St. Ignatius Loyola was that good people are not tempted grossly, as evil people are, by the glamor of sin—by wrongdoing that seems to offer pleasure, power, riches, or something like that. Good people are tempted subtly and deceptively, by what seems morally and spiritually good. But the end result is exactly the same: If they take the bait, they are destroyed by what they are attracted to. That's why Ignatius called it temptation."

"So what exactly is my temptation? I don't quite understand."

"Your temptation is to get worked up into this inner turmoil where you can't think and certainly have no leisure to love. You get talked into believing you're a terrible person, and you lose your faith and your hope, and you're so busy with your inner agony that you are no good to anyone. That's what I mean by destruction. The greater good gets wiped out."

"Now I think I'm beginning to see. I just never thought of it as temptation."

"That's what it is. It is incapacitating."

"So what do I do with it?"

"When you recognize it by the inner turmoil and confusion, and also by the paralysis of action to which it leads, pay no attention to it. It is not from God, even if at first it seems to be."

"I see what you mean now. I know that once I get into that whole syndrome and try to reason it out, I just get more and more tangled."

"Exactly. The only way to deal with it is to ignore it, and turn your attention to other things."

"It's really seductive, the whole rigmarole. So I've got something else I've got to work on."

****

In working with Cathy's depression, I see myself doing all that a comprehensive therapy suggests. I explore the various sources of the depression. I suggest making outer changes to reduce the negative and increase the positive in Cathy's life. I work on cognition, challenging false beliefs and unreasonable expectations. I suggest medication. And I do something more. I work with Cathy to integrate the spiritual dimension into this at every step. We simply bring it out into the open, because it is already there and is such a rich resource. It inserts our project into the larger framework of Cathy's ultimate meanings and values, brings it into alignment with her life's primary orientation, and taps her deepest motivation. This does not change the therapeutic steps at all, but it immensely enriches the entire process.

6.

Is This Marriage Over?

When Dave and Dana, a two-career couple from Los Angeles, packed up and moved to Seattle, it was the first time in their ten-year marriage that they had made a move in the interests of Dana's career. Dana had hated Los Angeles from the beginning, and resented being dragged there for the sake of Dave's job. She had borne with freeway and smog for five years, dutiful wife that she was, because Dave so enjoyed his work, the beach, his family, and his childhood friends. But her resentment just wouldn't go away. Before Los Angeles, it had been three years in San Francisco, again for the sake of a position Dave wanted. That move had pulled her away from her parents and the culture of New England. She was an only child, and her parents doted on her. She had found a very satisfying position right in Boston, her first after finishing medical school, where she and Dave had fallen in love. She had still not been able to shake the grief from all her losses. And she hated Dave at times for doing this to her.

Dave may have been insensitive, but he was not dumb. It dawned on him one day in Los Angeles that his marriage was coming apart. Dana was depressed and withdrawn. There was no sex, no affection, no fun. Their young daughter and son had begun showing signs of the damage of the unhappy family atmosphere. Dave loved his wife. When a friend of hers in Seattle told her of a superb job opening right down her line, and Dana relayed this to Dave with more energy in her voice than he had heard for a long, long time, Dave realized what he had to do. The only way to save his marriage was to let go of all that he had built for himself and make a fresh start in a distant city. When Dana was offered the job, he bade heavy farewells and they headed north.

Five months of life in the Pacific Northwest had elapsed when Dave and Dana came to see me. The happiness they'd hoped for still eluded them. Now it was Dave who was depressed. Though he had found a decent job, his losses lay heavy on his heart. Seattle's rain was getting to him. And Dana was furious, furious that Dave was depressed and that he seemed to be trying to sabotage this new venture so that they would have to go back to California. She had another ache as well. Her guilt was killing her. After ten years of marriage, she had finally asked for something for herself, and look what had come of it. Because of her "selfishness," Dave was miserable.

Identifying the Spiritual Dimension

I believe in marriage. There are marriages which destroy, and in those I do not believe. But most marriages create—or would if people would let them. They create two persons out of the raw materials originally presented, persons who emerge from the crucible of intimacy much *more* than they were when they unwittingly entered it, closer to being genuinely human, better at the art of loving—which from a Christian perspective is the whole purpose of life. But for this creation to take place, the two persons have to give themselves to the process. They have to submit to the truth that is being spoken in their ongoing dialogue, and follow it where it leads. Dave and Dana were in the crucible of intimacy now, and it was hot. But I believed God was with them, some of the things which needed to happen were happening, and they would come out the better for it.[1]

"I know you're both going through a really difficult time. I want you to reflect on it for a minute from a perspective you may or may not have considered. You both are Christian and you take your faith life seriously. What do you think the call of God to you might be in this painful struggle you are describing? I'm asking each of you, because the answer might be different for each."

There was a silence. It suggested they may not have thought about this before. Most people don't, even good Christians. When asked about the spiritual dimension of their marriage, all they can think of is, we have to stay together—and maybe we should go to church more often. Both responses miss the main point, which is how God is present and active in their ongoing relating, trying to do something with them.

"I know I've been selfish in our marriage and caused Dana a lot of suffering," Dave answered. "I think God wants me to make that right by accepting this whole new situation and making it work for Dana's sake. I definitely owe her one. I'm just having a terrible time doing it. I really miss California and everything I had there."

"I know I'm still dragging a sack of baggage from the past," Dana said. "I don't think I've ever forgiven Dave for what he's put me through, even though it's over now. I'm sure God wants me to forgive it, it's such a barrier between us." She paused. "And I guess I'm supposed to love him and support him now because he's going through such a hard time. I understand it; I've been there. But I don't like him at all right now. He's so depressed and angry and negative, all I want to do is get away from him. So I shut him out and isolate myself."

Nice answers both. Each showed a sense of what their vocation was, where they were failing, how they were being called to stretch and grow. They were hearing the deeper voice in the dialogue, and feeling the call to go with it, even though they hadn't moved very far yet. My question facilitated their identifying it and added spiritual motivation to the difficult work they knew they had to do. It located their struggle within the framework of the values which meant the most to them, the ultimate dedication of their lives.

Forgiveness

When they came the next time, I learned that very little had changed between them. There was still a freeze, and each walked alone. This wasn't going to be easy.

Dana spoke first. "It's the baggage I'm carrying from the past," she said. "It's like a wall between us. I mean all the resentment I built up against Dave because of the way he dragged me from place to place thinking only of himself. I still haven't been able to forgive it."

"I don't blame you," I said.

"The other thing is the terrible guilt I feel now. I see how depressed Dave is, and I say to myself, I did this to him. He must hate me, and that makes it hard for me to draw close. I feel like some kind of awful person."

Two thoughts crossed my mind as I listened. One was that Dana had *let* herself be dragged from place to place, or it would not have been possible. The other was that as soon as she asked for something for herself, she felt guilty. Both are clear symptoms of low self-esteem, and Dana, like so many women, had doubtless been conditioned to act and feel this way. A woman's role is to sacrifice herself for everyone else's happiness, the teaching goes. Now, whether you look at that therapeutically or theologically, it is an oppression that needs to be overturned. In pushing for Seattle, Dana had done the right thing, and her guilt was false guilt, a good person's temptation. When I commented on this to her, I was delighted to find Dave jumping in to help me, telling her he did not hold the move against her; he knew his grousing was his problem.

That left us with the issue of forgiveness. It was a major one for them. Dana had already named her resentment. Dave had his own grudge: Dana's coldness toward him and her stonewalling. They were hurting him deeply and bringing up a lot of anger. How could we deal with all this?

For forgiveness to occur, there usually has to be an apology. The offended party has to know that the offender has a sense of the pain their action caused, and is genuinely sorry. I asked Dana if she thought Dave was sorry for what he had done to her.

"No," she said. "He always explains it away. He tries to tell me all those moves were good for both of us. He just won't admit that he was really thinking only of himself, and the rest is all rationalization. I've given up arguing about it, because we just keep repeating ourselves. But the wall is still there."

We spent the next two sessions on this. I asked Dana to see if she could steer clear of criticism and blaming, and just talk about her feelings as she went over the chapters of their history. She did, and Dave was able to hear it all in a new way. I asked him to refrain from repeating all his reasons, and just join her in her feelings and try to respond to those. He caught the depth of her pain, was moved to admit it was mainly himself he had been thinking of, and apologized for all the suffering he had caused. The apology was heartfelt, and Dana heaved a sigh of relief and said maybe she could finally forgive.

Then we switched to his issue with her. Gradually Dave got beneath the outer crust of anger so habitual to him, and spoke from the valley of his pain. He showed the hurt and deprivation he felt as Dana consistently resisted his overtures to make love, spend time together, or even talk about their problems. She was visibly touched. She hadn't realized she was causing that much sorrow, and she apologized with much feeling. It seemed at last a breakthrough on both sides as far as the past was concerned. Wanting to build on it, I suggested they both ask God in their prayer over the following weeks to

give them a heart of forgiveness, which had so long seemed beyond
them. I also said that if they thought of other memories which were
blocking the flow of their love, they bring them back to the next session so we could work them through in the same way.

Therapy and spirituality blend in the process we had gone
through. It is therapy inasmuch as it aims to heal the wounded psyche,
lacerated with hurt and clouded with anger. It is also a spiritual exercise, the sort of thing religious groups do in rites of reconciliation.
The two merge nicely in the same basic procedure. What drawing out
the spiritual dimension adds is: motivation to do what is difficult, an
explicit seeking of God's assistance, and a recognition that in the end
forgiveness is a genuinely spiritual act.

Grieving Loss

Dana had had years to grieve her losses, and her work there was pretty
much done. Dave, on the other hand, had just entered a grieving
process, and he needed encouragement to let himself suffer the feelings
and share them with someone he felt safe with. Dana was not a good
choice for that, because she couldn't listen without feeling guilty and
defensive. Dave did most of his grieving with me in separate sessions.

"This is the hardest thing I think I've ever done. I had the perfect
setup in LA. My job required far fewer hours than I'm working now,
and I had some great colleagues. I've always loved the ocean, and
went to the beach a lot. My parents were right there. They're getting
older and my dad is not in very good health, so I spent as much time
with them as I could." He fell silent and stared into space. "Here it
seems like I'm working all the time. It's very hard to start over. And I
miss the sunshine terribly. This weather depresses me. The other thing
is the loneliness. I have no friends here. I reach out to Dana and she
pulls away. About the only thing I have is the kids."

All I could do was empathize. There was no escaping the
anguish of his losses. All of us go through a grieving process many
times in life, any time we lose something dear. We feel numb or dis-
believing at first, then angry, sad, sometimes self-blaming, and fearful
as we face the future. These feelings keep cycling through, now one,
now the other, until they begin gradually to abate. Slowly we become
able to let go and move on. The psyche, by its own inner dynamism,

heals itself—if only we face rather than deny our loss, allow the feel-ings to swirl rather than stuff them down, and share our pain with someone who can offer understanding and support.

Spirituality can be a tremendous assist in this process, an addi-tional support, a larger framework of meaning within which we can bear a particular loss.[2] People in grief often pray that God simply be with them in a special way and help them bear their pain without going to pieces, and they often do feel a support. Grief thus becomes an occasion for deepening their relationship with God. But sometimes God, too, seems far away.

"I know you've suggested I pray through this, and share it all with God. But I feel as if God has abandoned me. There's just nothing there. I don't know if I even believe in God anymore."

I shared my faith conviction that God was with him even if he could not feel it now, fully realizing my words might sound empty to him. But it sometimes helps to hear that somebody else still believes. Often it is only *after* a crisis that we can see how God was with us.

"I'm beginning to see this whole experience as an immense test of faith for me. I'm letting go of my whole life, it seems like. What an act of trust. Will God give me a future? Can God bring me back to life? It certainly does not seem so as I survey the barren landscape of my existence. I guess I have to believe in the resurrection. That's not so easy when you're hanging on the cross."

And so the grieving process continued. In addition to our work together, Dave found much support in a Jewish friend in LA, with whom he had several long talks on the phone.

Risking All

For all our efforts, things seemed to get worse for Dave and Dana. At least they got no better. Dave continued depressed and pining for California. Dana continued to withhold herself from him, disgusted and afraid he would any day announce he simply could not make it here and was going back with or without her. I was genuinely afraid a divorce might be shaping up. They had allowed the deterioration for so many years, and now this crisis was stretching the weakened fibers to the snapping point. Could it be that nothing would come of Dave's agreeing to Seattle to atone for the past, their honest attempts at forgiveness, and Dave's earnest effort to let go of some of his dearest possessions? Or might the tide still turn?

Sometimes therapy is just sitting helplessly by as a profound inner upheaval plays itself out. About all the therapist can do is provide a place where the protagonist(s) can freely sweat and groan and feel supported as well as believed in while they fight it through. Then it is the *therapist's* faith that is tested. I often felt this way as I sat with this couple, unable to do much though I kept searching for approaches, caring for the two of them and clinging to hope. My office was at least a place where they could talk; they talked very little at home. What seemed to be holding them together during this time was a resource more robust than therapy—their two children, whom both dearly loved and neither was willing to part with.

There was another bit of data which kept me encouraged, and I remarked on it. Both were overworking at their new positions, and their time together was at once very limited and fraught with tension. But they took breaks in the form of mini-vacations, sometimes in, sometimes out of, state. They always came back reporting they'd had a great time. It seemed that as soon as they got away from work and Seattle, a completely different spirit took over and they genuinely enjoyed one another. They even made love. This convinced me it was the difficult transition, not the marriage itself, that was the main problem.

But now we were in a phase where for several weeks they seemed to be merely stuck, both unhappy, nothing moving. I thought it time for a major push.

"Here's what I see," I said, and I went to a small blackboard where, in my best artistic style, I drew a crude fork in the road. "You're standing at this fork," I said, "too scared to move, and so you're not budging. This way lies divorce. Dave goes back to LA, Dana stays here, and you have a legal battle for custody of the children, who lose no matter who wins. That way lies a brand new marriage, and it has to be lived in Seattle. The old marriage will no longer work. If you go the route of the new marriage in Seattle, each of you has to die—which is, of course, why you hesitate. Dave, you have to die to California's sunshine and all that it warms, and get both feet into your marriage and your job here, though neither is what you'd like it to be. Ouch! Dana, you have to die to your dream of what you thought your marriage would be, let go of your resentments about the past, and put your whole heart into loving this man just as he is. To make it harder, you have to love him right now, while he's at his most unlovable.

"This is a huge risk for both of you. Dana, you have to love Dave right in his grief and his ambivalence, *before* he comes out of them. It's a gamble, because he might still bolt for California. But the only way he can let go and invest here is if you love him and remarry him now. It was to remarry you that he came here; if there is no marriage, why should he stay?

"Dave, you have to commit to Seattle and Dana before you know for sure she'll love you or that you can build a good life here. If you don't, how can you expect her to commit to you? You have to say goodby to the past once and for all; there's no way the two of you can go back there, even though Dana keeps saying you'll probably have to. It would be a disaster for your marriage. Dana needs a sign from you that you really mean to settle here. You've got to make some friends, get into some activities, embrace your work in a way that shows you're in for the long haul. And by the way, I think all this talk about Seattle's gloomy skies is a metaphor for the absence of Dana's love. That is the sunshine you really miss."

They were listening. It took me only two or three minutes to say all this, but it felt as if the clock were stopped much longer. I was taking strong positions and asking a lot, but they knew they were stuck and that the issues were life and death. It was time for decision.

"We're talking bedrock spirituality here," I said. "This is a plunge with no assurance but raw trust in God. It's a death. And both of you have to do it, because if either of you holds back, it won't work."

That was when the tide began to turn. Dana started showing Dave some affection, and it softened his hard edge. Dave gave evidence that he was embracing Seattle as his new home, and Dana relaxed and opened even more. Dave still struggled with his grief, and Dana still lost patience with him sometimes. But they had definitely turned a corner, and they evidenced more peace and closeness after that.

An appointment a couple of months later coincided with Dave's birthday. They were looking forward to dinner out and a special evening after our session. I didn't want to get into any discussion that might cast a pall over the celebration, so I chose to go with the birthday energy instead. I suggested an exercise my wife and I have often used in leading marriage enrichment days for couples. I asked them to turn to each other, and name qualities they loved and cherished in one another. They entered into it with remarkable warmth.

"Dave, I love your good looks. You have a great sense of humor (when you're not down in the dumps), and I always enjoy it. You're a really competent doctor, and I admire that in you. You're a wonderful father to our children. I love the special events and vacations you dream up for us. And I appreciate your being willing to come to Seattle for me."

"Dana, you're a beautiful woman, inside and out. I love your New England accent and your warm, beautiful smile. I love the way you reach out to me and support me. You often encourage me when I'm down. You're a wonderful lover. I love your spontaneity and energy. You've been loyal, and I haven't been easy to be loyal to. You're a great mother."

And so the energy flowed, refreshing their spirits.

Comfort and challenge, the two creative hands of God. This couple had challenged each other profoundly, and were growing now because of their response to that challenge. But now on Dave's birthday, they were comforting one another, incarnating God's other creative energy, the one that soothes, relaxes, and expands. It is an equally potent agent of growth.

7.

How Could God Allow This?

Jim was a wiry high school theology teacher in his forties. He had told me over the phone that he was the victim of both physical and sexual abuse as a child, and that he was in therapy for that. What he wanted was someone who could work with him simultaneously on the spiritual issues involved. His therapist had suggested me. I had not been in this sort of division-of-labor situation since my years as a Jesuit spiritual director, when some of my directees had been in therapy. I agreed to work with him.

"I can't feel the love of God," Jim said. "I think I believe in it, but I've never felt it. I was hoping you could help me with that."

Jim had grown up in a family in which both parents beat him until he was too big for that to be possible anymore. His father used to keep him in suspense over it, promising it at the end of the day so he could think about it. There was plenty to think about, because Dad used a belt and was in no hurry to get it over with. Jim used to pray in his room that God would somehow save him, but God never did. He also prayed that he would get his teddy bear back, which Dad had thrown out the car window one day when Jim was about four because he had said or done something wrong in the back seat, but that prayer was not answered either. Jim's parents were both pillars of their local church. At 13, Jim repudiated his faith. At 16, he left home for good. He used drugs heavily through high school and early college. The scars of his childhood were still visible.

Jim related these events in a matter of fact tone which told me he would have some work to do in therapy. There the core task would be to relive the traumatic events and let himself feel the awful feelings for the first time and unburden himself to someone—something he could not do as a child in the original environment. Jim still held the feelings deep inside, so far down he would have difficulty for awhile accessing them. But our work lay in a different realm.

"I can certainly understand your wanting to feel God's love," I said. "The problem is, I can't make it happen. Neither can you. It's

God's gift. We can ask for it, and open ourselves to it, but we can't make it happen."

"But that is what I feel I most need."

"It is at least what you would most like, and I understand that perfectly. And, like you, I'm inclined to think it would really help a lot. But in spite of all its desirability, it is really not the substance of the spiritual life. In fact, it seems to be more common in the early stages of the spiritual life than in the more mature."

"Really?"

"Yes. Maybe it's something like the first flush of being in love with someone, before it settles down into a quiet commitment." And then I added something, because it is so easy for someone in Jim's position to think they are the only one who lacks what everyone else has. "As a matter of fact, Jim, I'd like to feel the love of God more myself," I added. "I've felt it on only a few occasions in my life. Most of the time I have to just live by faith."

Jim looked surprised as I said these things, possibly also disappointed. Finally he said, "Maybe feeling God's love is not the real issue. Sometimes I wonder if there *is* a God. When I look back at my childhood, I just can't understand how a God of love could allow what happened to me. What a world."

The Problem of Evil

He swallowed hard, looked at the floor, and slowly began. "When I was about eight, my mother and I spent a night at my uncle's house. We played games during the evening. I felt a little afraid of my uncle, but there didn't seem to be any reason to. I was assigned a room by myself in the back of the house. Sometime during the night, I woke suddenly to find my uncle bending over me. He told me not to make a sound, and raped me brutally. He told me if I ever told, he'd kill me. The next morning my mother discovered the blood on my pajamas and on the bed and asked me what had happened. Scared as I was, I couldn't think of anything but to tell the truth. She took hold of my arm and looked me hard in the eye. 'If anything like that happened it was your fault,' she said, 'and don't you ever say a word about this again! Do you hear me?' Then she slapped me in the face, and left the room. We never spoke of it again." Now Jim was having difficulty holding the feelings at bay. So was I. I was horrified at what he had related, and I shook my head again and again in amazement. No wonder this man had trouble believing in the love of God.

We stayed awhile with the experience and the feelings that accompanied it, which Jim so needed at last to feel and share. Then we came back to the theological question which troubled him.

"Jim, you know you're asking the hardest question there is: How can a God who is supposedly good allow things like this to happen? You're theologically educated, and have seen all the best answers the human mind has been able to come up with. You know that even taken together, they do not really explain it. God remains utterly beyond us. Like Job, who wrestled with this dilemma very personally, we simply do not understand, and we cry out into the dreadful silence. The problem of evil has been the greatest challenge to my faith too. Every day in this office, I hear new horror stories. And yet I believe." I knew he knew that. I also knew that the mere fact of that, and the way I would deal with him, would carry more weight than any verbal testimony I would give.

"Well, what sense do you make of the dreadful mess of the world and God's supposed love and power?"

It was obvious that the man who sat before me was not only wounded, but very intelligent and reflective. "For me, Jim, the best stab at the mystery comes from process theology. Do you know anything of Alfred North Whitehead's thought?"

"Not really."

"Well, he's been very influential in twentieth-century philosophical theology, challenging the classical thought of Thomas Aquinas with a very different way of looking at reality, based in our contemporary experience of evolution and of the interrelatedness of all things. Anyway, when he comes to the problem of evil, what he stresses is that God chose to create a world genuinely distinct from self and therefore genuinely free. That choice limits what God can do in the management of the world. There is some measure of freedom in all things, and it is, of course, particularly broad at the human level. God continually invites and draws all things toward the good ends God envisions, but God neither coerces nor forcibly prevents, always respecting the freedom of creation. That means we are at liberty to do what is evil—and we do plenty of it, as history shows. It leaves a trail of destruction.

"In some ways that is a better explanation than the one that God is really in control of everything, which leaves you wondering why so many things seem to go so tragically yet God does nothing about it. But if we go with Whitehead's presentation of the matter, I'm not sure God's experiment is working. The world is still the same mess.

"I've often had the same impression. So where is God? How does God work with such a system? Whitehead's answer is that God is still faithful and active, always working with us to salvage all that can be salvaged, bringing all possible good out of evil. Whitehead has a wonderful saying that goes something like this:

> God is the poet of the world, with tender patience leading
> it with the divine vision of beauty, goodness, and truth.

Whitehead's God is not the all-powerful monarch of classical tradition, but rather a loving visionary, like an artist, holding up an ideal of beauty and working to help us realize it. In Whitehead's view, God struggles just as we do, and God suffers along with us. The whole creation is in process, and God is no less in process.

"It's a little bit scary to think of a world God doesn't fully control. But that does correspond with our experience, doesn't it? It is too great an affront to the mind to think that the way this world actually goes is all God's will. And they used to add that God sends us our sufferings as some sort of test. That kind of God has always seemed terribly cruel to me. The idea that God does not will our sufferings, but grieves with us in them, and works with us to turn them to good, is a lot more palatable."

"I think so too. Like you, I was schooled in the old tradition, but have found this reading of the matter far more consistent with my adult experience. I think of God as a great gambler, because I believe God cares greatly about us yet has placed us in a free system in which we can not only be victimized, but we ourselves can victimize. We carry a lot of responsibility for the direction of the world's development."

"I'd like to explore Whitehead's thought a little more. What would you suggest I read?"

I suggested Cobb and Griffin's summary, *Process Theology*, and, specifically on the problem of God and human suffering, Kushner's *When Bad Things Happen to Good People*.[1] Kushner does not explicitly call his theology process, but that is what it is.

"I want to come back to something I mentioned earlier, Jim. I told you I hear a lot of horror stories in this office. I think the reason why I can hear accounts of injustice and human pain every day and find my faith somehow strengthened rather than weakened is that I can so plainly see the goodness of the person telling the story. They have not only survived what was visited on them, but they have somehow become the person they are through it. They are beautiful."

"I know what you mean. I do quite a bit of counseling myself, and I've felt the same thing."

"What may surprise you is that I see it in you, Jim. I don't mean to minimize the tragedies of your childhood at all. But if we took the sufferings and struggles of your life away, would we still have *you*?"

He laughed. "I don't know what you're seeing. I don't see much. And I sure am pissed at my uncle and at my dad, and at my mother, and I've been pissed at God for a long time too."

I smiled, and didn't argue. I had no wish to explain his feelings away. They needed scope at last to be and to be heard. But here was a man whose substance impressed me. He was married, devoted to his family, especially tender with his three children, passing on none of the abuse that had been heaped on him. His work was teaching theology and counseling, and he was much sought out by students. For years he had been living a life that made a difference, and it had grown out of the things he suffered.

I could let his angry feelings be. I was seeding ideas whose sprouts would appear—if they appeared at all—only after he had walked with them awhile. Therapeutically, it is far more important that our experience be understood and accepted than that our minds be given an explanation. And yet if we have an interest in living by faith, and many people do, our vision of faith has to mature along with the rest of our experience. Our minds have needs along with our hearts. And Jim, who was doing therapy elsewhere, had come to me precisely for the spiritual dimension.

Healing of Memories

In a later session, we were again talking about the years of physical abuse Jim had suffered at the hands of his parents. It had made his entire childhood a very dark, anguished experience, and the taste of it seemed still to linger in his mouth. One of the things I often do in treating painful memories is use visualization. After enough healing work has taken place to make this possible, I have the person return in imagination to the scene of the trauma, accompanied this time by Jesus (or some other trusted religious figure, e.g., Mary). Usually, the original scene is somehow transformed by what Jesus does with it. I was thinking of going this route with Jim because I remembered what he had said about never having experienced God's love. Visualization is an experience; it involves and has impact on the total person. I introduced the idea to Jim, and he was willing to try it.

I took a few minutes to relax him and get him internally focused. Then I invited him to be a little boy again and return in imagination to the home of his childhood, and see and smell and feel the place. His eyes were closed, but we dialogued.

"I can see it so clearly, and I have an awful feeling in the pit of my stomach."

I did not want to leave him long in that. I just wanted him really to be there. "Now invite Jesus to join you there. When he comes, notice how he looks and what he does." And I left a silence.

"I'm in the sandbox in the backyard and he comes to me there." Pause. "He likes me." Pause. "He gets in the sandbox and we play together."

I'm listening with delight. This is exactly what needs to happen. "Let yourself really enjoy that, Jim. Take some time with it." And I leave several minutes. Then I ask, "What's happening now."

"He's just holding me."

Wonderful. I want to let the feeling deepen. "Notice what that feels like. Let it sink way down into you."

"He tells me he will be my friend forever."

"Beautiful. Take it in."

After a few more minutes, I invited him to bring the scene to a close. When he came out of his trance, I suggested he return to the experience in his prayer during the next week, to enhance its working in him.

When he came the next time, he said he had not been able to recapture the feeling too well in his prayer, but that some sense of God's love for him had remained. I told him the follow-up was usually not as potent as the original experience, but it was still worth doing. Then he told me he had prayed that his sense of God's love be increased.

Then the skeptic in him spoke. "But how do I know that visualization isn't just self-deception?"

"How do you mean?"

"I mean, how do I know it isn't something I just cook up all by myself—wishful thinking without any reality?"

This fellow asked good questions. I had to think about it a minute. "I do a lot of visualization with people," I said, "and, as with you, I guide it minimally. What strikes me again and again is how uncanny yet apt what happens is. It is something neither I nor the other person could have 'cooked up' nearly so ingeniously. Take what happened to you. If I had said, 'Imagine Jesus and you playing together in the sandbox,' or 'Imagine Jesus holding you in his arms,' even if you had been able to imagine that, you would have come out thinking it was all my idea. But I didn't create it at all—beyond suggesting you invite Jesus to come and then watch what he does. And I don't think you cooked it up because it was precisely what you have not experienced and would be inclined to think impossible for yourself. Also, what typically happens, as with you, is something very much in harmony with what the Bible tells us of God's love. For all these reasons, I am convinced these experiences are genuinely graced. This sort of focused visualization exercise heightens our attunement to the God who already dwells within, enabling God to do what God always wants to do for us."

"You make a pretty good case. I just wanted to be sure. You said you wanted to do another one today?"

"All right. Let's do it. Take a few minutes to relax and get internally focused."

When he was ready, I asked him to be a little boy again and go back home. It is that "inner child" who carries the emotional burden and needs the healing.

"I am alone in the house. My parents are gone. I'm very lonely and sad. And scared."

Again he is in touch with the original experience. I do not want to reinforce that, but only to make sure he has really reentered that space inside himself.

"Ask Jesus to come to you there. When he comes, take a moment really to see him." Pause.

"He is with me." Silence. "We're walking through the house. We find abuse in absolutely every room." Silence. I wait. "Jesus takes me in his arms and comforts me." Several minutes pass as I let him savor this experience. It is the graced transformation of the original trauma.

"What's happening now?"

"I'm asking him to take me away." I wonder how Jesus will handle that. It is out of my control. Pause. "He says it doesn't work that way, that I have to stay. But he says he loves me and will come back." Pause. "He's telling me that he hurts with me."

Again I am struck by the uncanny originality and aptitude of what happens. What a wonderful thing for Jesus to say to him. It means much more than if I had told him I hurt with him, or even said Jesus hurts with him. It is the wounded, scared child, still very much alive within Jim, who speaks and acts, and it is to him that Jesus accommodates. I let Jim assimilate the experience before suggesting he bring the scene to a close. When he comes out of the trance, he says, "I think maybe I'm beginning to experience God's love." Bravo!

The Issue of Forgiveness

Several months had gone by, and in his other therapy Jim had relived the traumatic events of his childhood in more detail, written about them, drained more of the anguish. Now the question of forgiveness began to exercise his Christian mind.

"What am I supposed to do about forgiveness? Jesus was so clear on it—70 times 7, and so forth—and he practiced what he preached. But I'm having, if you'll pardon the expression, a hell of a time with it. My parents have never indicated the slightest remorse. When I tried talking with them about all this, they told me I was making a mountain out of a molehill. They totally denied most of it, and expressed shock and hurt that I had such negative feelings toward them. The uncle who abused me is dead. Never once, while he lived, did he mention that horrible night that he violated me. And now I'm just supposed to forgive all this? It has ruined my life!"

Jim's feelings were completely justified. And forgiveness cannot be hurried in cases like this. But we were both aware of Jesus' teaching on forgiveness, and I knew besides that harbored resentment exacts a price. It takes its toll on the psyche and even the body. To answer his difficult question, we would have to do some puzzling out loud. First I wanted to support his feelings.

"You have every reason to feel as you do. And I just can't imagine Jesus, or anybody else who cares about you, telling you not to feel that way, or in some simplistic fashion saying, 'Just forgive it, Jim. Move on.' " He seemed to relax. "As you know, it is absolutely essential to your therapy that you get the blame for what happened off yourself and put it where it belongs. And since God wants you to heal, then God would support your anger and resentment as a step in that process. So Jesus' words can't possibly mean 'Stuff it all back down and go embrace those people.' "

"No. That would be impossible at this point anyway. So I'm left with the question, how do I live Jesus' teaching?"

"Let's see if we can puzzle it out together. One way to begin is by naming some things forgiveness is not—courses of action which are either impossible or unhealthy, but with which forgiveness is sometimes confused."

"Well, I'm sure it can't mean condoning, or even minimizing, the evil that was done. I've tried minimizing it, and it won't go down."

"I agree completely."

"And I don't see how it can mean forgetting. We've all heard the adage 'Forgive and forget,' but how can we forget the greatest injuries of our lives? I'd need a lobotomy."

"I'm with you there too. And I'd add another item, though it does not apply so much to your case. Forgiveness can't mean allowing the bad behavior to continue, the way the spouses of alcoholics or batterers sometimes do."

"Yes, I agree with that too. Actually, one way your idea applies is that I'm trying not to let my parents abuse me anymore in any way, just out of respect for myself."

"That's wonderful, another sign of the great progress you have made."

"So what is forgiveness?"

"I think it means not holding it against them anymore, not keeping them reminded of it, not trying to exact a recompense."

"Of course, I can't do that with my uncle anyway. There I guess it just means letting go, letting him be dead, leaving the whole matter to God. With my parents, what you are saying sounds right. It's hard, because they've never even acknowledged that it happened. I still can't accept that."

"You know how I think it will finally happen, Jim? My hunch is that someday—not now, now would be the wrong time—someday down the road God will put it in your heart to forgive, and you will just do it. The bad things your parents and your uncle did to you just won't matter so much anymore. You will have healed and come to know that you are OK and that these past events aren't hurting you. I don't think you have to strain at this now. God will give it in time, and that will be the final stage in your healing."

"I must say it sounds preposterous today that I will ever be able to do that. I'll have to take your word for it. I can see that carrying around the rage I'm feeling now for the rest of my life would make all happiness impossible. But I can't seem to get rid of it right now."

I was glad to hear he knew he could not hold a grudge forever. But rage held center stage for now, it really belonged there, and nothing would dislodge it until it burned itself out. I cannot imagine the God who designed our emotional system wanting us to do violence to the design. Nature would take its course, and it would all work out.

The Question of Permanent Damage

Jim's therapy was progressing nicely. One of the clear signs of that was how enlivened he was. His fine mind and spiritual sensitivity had been evident from the outset. What was new was all the energy. He had gotten his emotional life back, and it animated him wonderfully. I remarked on this one day.

"If this is what it is to feel," he responded with a laugh, "you can have it. I've got a lot of new emotions all right, but they're mostly painful. This is progress? This is what I'm putting out my life savings for?"

We both laughed. Jim had a lot of personality, and a great sense of humor. "It's wonderful to see you more and more alive," I said. "It's as if you've had circulation restored to your limbs, and you can run and jump again. It's interesting how our emotional life is a totality. If we numb the pain, we numb the joy too. I know you've got a lot of agony right now, but it's just a season. The weather will change."

"I'm not so sure about that. I think I've got some permanent damage I'm not going to be able to eradicate."

"What do you mean?"

"For one thing, I see the world very negatively. I expect the worst, always have. For another, I don't trust anybody. Then, I don't feel much joy, ever. It's interesting we're talking about this. My therapist told me I should start cultivating the positive feelings now, noticing the beauty around me, enjoying the little things. That's really hard for me. I've been trying it, but I'm just not getting much. I wonder if I have any capacity for joy. That's why I'm saying I've got some deep damage, and I don't know if it's ever going to heal."

"I really like your therapist's assignment. It's an excellent focus. Sounds as if it is going to take some practice, but I'm sure you'll get results if you stay at it. As far as the damage is concerned, I know the abuse has hurt you. But I think it has also blessed you. I've always loved that story of Jacob wrestling with an angel all through the night (Gen 32). It left with him a wounded hip—but also with a blessing. So I would like to add an assignment of my own. What I'd like you to do for next time is a full assessment of yourself, listing both the negative and positive qualities which you have as a result of the childhood you had." We talked a little more about this task, and concluded our session.

He came the next time with a far richer list than I'd expected. Usually people come with a list far better developed on the negative side than on the positive, and we have to work together to balance out the ledger. Jim showed a good awareness of his strengths. I added another trait or two on the basis of my knowledge of him. He was already aware how gently and care-fully he parented his own children, and how much they loved him in return. He recognized the depth of his compassion for others. He acknowledged his sense of humor. He knew his passionate dedication to justice, and his empathy with injustice's victims in any situation. He was cognizant of the inner and outer resourcefulness he had developed during his long childhood loneliness. He recognized his popularity with students, and admitted that though he had his difficulties with God he had chosen to be a teacher of Christian theology and a counselor, and felt good about what he had been able to do for others.

Even his negative list was not as long as people sometimes make them. I was glad, and pointed out that even the so-called bad traits—such as his slowness to trust—had a positive side as well. As we concluded, Jim seemed strengthened by the whole exercise.

"I'm not so sure about all that permanent damage you were talking about, Jim. In fact," I said, "I think what we've gone over today is cause for celebration. So I hope you will do some little ritual of celebration before we meet again." What I had in mind was that he treat himself in some small way, or share with a friend this entire therapy experience and especially the goodness he had unearthed in himself. Jim's understanding proved to be a little different, which was all to the good.

A Ritual of Healing

Two weeks went by before Jim's next appointment. He opened by telling me about "the ritual."

"I had a devil of a time coming up with a ritual of celebration. I couldn't think of anything. Then it came to me that a ritual is essentially a physical analogy. So I asked myself what it was I sought a physical analogy for, and I realized it was good coming out of evil. Well, we live out in the country, and have a pretty good-sized backyard. Ever since we got the place, I've been bothered by a clump of old tree roots which are an eyesore back there, but I've never quite gotten myself to take them on. And right near them is an old compost pile the previous owner built, but he didn't do it right and it never worked. It was just a mess of plastic sheets, refuse, and what not. Well, I decided that area of the yard was my symbol of evil, and my ritual would be to bring good out of it.

"I asked my kids if they wanted to help me. I remembered how my dad always forced me to work with him, and I didn't want to do that to my kids. I just told them what I was planning, and said they'd be welcome to join me, even if they just wanted to stand around and talk. They came, and they helped. We talked quite a bit, too, as we went along. I dug out all those old roots, and we cut them up. We took apart the compost pile and leveled the ground. I'm still stiff and sore, but we actually had a good time doing it. It was important to me that the ritual involve my body, since so much of the abuse came through my body. A ritual using mere words would have been too easy.

"Then my wife and I went out and bought several flowering trees, and all of us worked together to plant them."

I was amazed and moved as I listened to this. This was a brilliant piece of self-therapy. He really knew how to do a ritual of healing.

"The work took several days. The day we finished planting the trees, we had a dinner of celebration. I had a ten-year-old bottle of French wine I'd been saving for God-knows-what. I had caught and frozen a big salmon last summer, and we thawed that. My wife made a pie, the kids, favorite dessert, and we bought some ice cream. We lit a candle, and we gave thanks for all our blessings. We even let the kids have seconds on dessert, which we don't usually do, because this was a very special occasion. As we ate, we looked out the window and enjoyed the fruits of our labors. What was an eyesore is now probably the most beautiful part of the yard." He laughed.

"Did you tell the kids what this was all about?" I asked.

"I didn't tell them about the sexual abuse. They're still too young for that. I did tell them how my parents abused me physically, and how I am getting help in counseling for that now and it is healing. So to a large extent they knew what this was all about."

I congratulated him enthusiastically. This was the best healing ritual I had ever heard of, and the new grove of flowering trees would stand for the rest of Jim's life as a memorial of how he and God had brought good out of evil. I felt like having a little champagne myself.

This was not the end of our work, but it was the heart of it. We had met about twenty times, over the course of a year.

If I had been the principal therapist, I would have done what that therapist was doing—having Jim relive his painful past and bleed out the feelings so they could heal. When a child falls and bruises his knee, he runs to a parent crying. He is picked up and held, his wound taken seriously and treated if necessary, his hurt feelings met with compassion and care. He is assured that everything will be all right. Tears dried, he goes off again to play. It is done. The unhappy incident will simply fade. But suppose the child has no one to go to with his pain and alarm. Or worse, suppose his parents are the cause of them. Then there is nowhere to turn. He has to deal with it all by himself, and he lacks the resources. He has to hold in the feelings, unresolved. To go on, he has to wall them off from awareness, because he can neither express nor live with them. And so they are stored in the cellar, and there they accumulate, and from there they continue to influence his mood and behavior indefinitely—until what should have taken place at the time of the occurrence can finally take place in a therapeutic setting. The inner child needs reparenting.

If I had been the principal therapist, that is what I would have done. But I would have spoken of the spiritual dimension of the issues as well, since I see that dimension as highly relevant and very helpful. With another therapist working on the case, it was merely the proportions that changed somewhat. I worked mainly on the spiritual—the question of God's love, the problem of evil, the spiritual healing of memories, the issue of forgiveness, and the truth of God's gracing of the struggles of our lives. But this spiritual work, too, is therapy. Sound spiritual guidance is always therapeutic. Then, too, Jim and I regularly dealt with the reliving and processing of the past, simply because it kept coming up. And I was an additional healing presence or sacrament in Jim's life—no small bonus since it is nurturing personal relationships, more than any techniques, that ultimately heal us. Jim was reciprocal gift and grace to me.

There is a paradox in this case. Jim knew as much theology as I did, and doubtless explained and did for others the very things I explained and did for him. So why did he need me? Because in our own regard, we are poor judges and hamstrung ministers of the gospel. In the end, the human being is essentially a social being. In the Roman Catholic sacramental system, the priest, who is minister of the sacraments, does not reconcile or anoint himself. He needs someone else to do it for him.

I had occasion to talk with Jim by phone some nine months after we concluded our work. He told me he was doing very well. And he volunteered a reflection. "You know," he said, "the best thing you gave me was not a new image of God. That was helpful, but what has mattered more is that you gave me a new image of myself. You told me I was a masterpiece—that given my background it was amazing what kind of a person I had become. That is what has made the most difference in the way I feel." It is all a paradox. We think we are doing one thing, and we are really doing something else. Ultimately it is God who is quietly at work accomplishing the divine purpose.[2]

8.

The Woman Who Was Selfish

I first met Amy in a theology course I taught to graduate students in ministry in the midwest. A few years after she got her master's, she moved to Seattle and took a job in one of the parishes as religious education coordinator. I saw her a time or two at social gatherings. I still hardly knew who she was, and had no notion of the burden she carried in her heart. Then one day she called and asked if she could see me. It was an obviously troubled Amy who presented herself.

"My husband has a rare neurological disease. He's had it since the first year of our marriage, and we've been married 18 years. The disease affects him both mentally and physically, bit by bit destroying him. The first couple of years of our marriage he managed to keep working full time. Then he had to cut to part time. For the last 12 years he hasn't been able to work at all. He's at home all the time, and I'm the caretaker. He's in a wheelchair now, and his hands shake so badly I have to spoonfeed him. I have to help him to the bathroom. I have to bathe him. I have to do everything for him. Many medications have been tried. Nothing has worked. He keeps going down, but slowly. He may live another 30 years."

I sat there taking this in, trying to imagine what such a life would be like for each of them. Her tone, weight, posture told me what it was doing to her. The blow had fallen in the very first year of their marriage, and since then 18 years had gone by. Wow. I had noticed on the registration form that they had a daughter 17.

"I work all day. His mother comes over, or sometimes a nurse, to take care of his needs. I think I could bear with it if it were just a matter of taking care of him. But he's very angry, and he complains all the time. No matter what I do for him, it's never enough. If I have to stay late at work, or have an evening meeting, he complains. When I am at home, he wants my attention all the time. He interrupts when I try to read. He is jealous of all my relationships. He thinks I am having an affair. Sometimes I wish I were. He frequently calls me at work, and it is always to grumble about something."

I could feel my heart growing heavy as I listened. What a dreadful existence for both of them. And there seemed to be no escape.

"Legally we are married—but I certainly don't feel married. There is no way he can be a husband to me. He can't share with me or support me, and the extent of the fun we can have together is playing cards in the evening. He can't help me with decisions; he just doesn't have the mental capacity anymore to make good judgments. I have to carry it all alone. He is not my husband. He is my child, and I am his mother. Yet he wants sex all the time, and can't understand why I refuse. But I just can't bring myself to it; we don't have that kind of relationship. He tells me I'm selfish. Am I selfish? I resent him, and I resent the whole situation. I have so much anger."

A Burden Shared

When I hear a story like this, I always hope it is true that people are helped simply by sharing their burden with someone, because I can think of so little to say which might lighten it. Then I reflect further. What is she really asking of me? She *knows* I cannot take it away, yet she seeks me out. She comes to me as a therapist, because she probably wonders if there is something wrong with her (so angry, so depressed, so sexless), and she comes to me as a spiritual director because she wants some help putting her plight into a faith perspective ("I'm an awful person, aren't I? I don't have any faith at all, do I?"). So, over and above empathy and support, I can give her back some assurance in both those areas.

"What an impossible situation, Amy. It must be awful for both of you. I can understand Bob's anger and need; and I can just as easily understand your feeling overwhelmed, powerless, and resentful. It is a tragic predicament for both of you.

"I cannot imagine anyone in your situation not feeling angry. It's not fair. I am sure you do a great deal for your husband, and it sounds as if you get very little thanks for it. It also seems that, in his pain and fear, he would completely take over your life if he could. How could you not resent that and get very angry at him sometimes, even though you do care about him? What I'm saying is that your feelings about all this are perfectly natural and normal. They are not blameworthy at all."

She visibly relaxed. I had neither criticized her nor given some easy advice.

"Amy, there is no way you or I with our human minds can make sense of the situation you describe. It is simply incomprehensible to us. Bob doesn't get it. You don't get it. I don't either. As I watch Jesus in the gospels in his encounters with suffering people, he never says, 'God sent this to you,' or 'This is good for you,' or 'This is a special sign of God's love.' He offers no explanation or justification of it. He simply acts to alleviate suffering as much as he can. And he bears his own with dignity, putting his trust in God. That seems to be all any of us can do."

I stopped. She was silent.

"But I have so little faith," she said. "Sometimes I wonder if I believe in God at all. I am certainly not patient. I really feel like a bad person—so angry, so selfish, so despairing."

Both therapeutically and spiritually, I believe the best thing I can offer Amy is to accept her as she is, to let her express the feelings she hates but which are there anyway, to let her be imperfect without laying any judgment on her, to be with her in her struggle, and to refrain from suggesting some simplistic solution because there is no solution, simple or otherwise.

I would see Amy off and on over the next twelve years. Rarely did she come more than once a month. Sometimes three or even six months would go by without a visit. She came when her circumstances became unbearable. Then she needed support and the restoration of perspective. She needed to unburden herself, to vent her anger and exhaustion, to "confess her sins," and to hear someone outside the situation validate her feelings and reassure her she was doing as well with an extremely difficult situation as anyone could do. One day she named the function I performed in her life. "You are my anchor," she said.

How Much Is Enough?

In the course of twelve years' dialogue with a person about any core struggle which is ongoing, you have essentially the same conversation many times. Yet it is always somehow useful. Each time you come to it, each of you is a little different, and so are the circumstances.

Several years after we had begun, after a five month span without a session, Amy came in with some news.

"About a month ago, I put Bob in a nursing home," she said sadly. "He needed more and more care, day and night. I reached a breaking point. I couldn't keep caring for him and continue to do my job, and, of course, I have no choice but to work. It was the only thing I could think of to do. I guess I've always known it would come to this some day. But it was an agonizing decision."

I could see in her face what a difficult decision it was, and how her pain continued even though she no longer had immediate responsibility for him.

"He hates me for what I've done. He hates everything about the nursing home, even though they give him excellent care and the staff are really very solicitous. He calls me and keeps threatening to come home. I don't know what to do. I feel so guilty."

"I think you made the right decision, Amy. There is really no doubt in my mind. You kept him as long as you could, possibly even longer. The type of care he needs now you simply cannot give, though part of you wants to. It would destroy you, and still not suffice for him."

She paused as she studied me. "I guess that's what I needed to hear from you, or from someone. It's so hard to be objective in a situation like this. But I respect your judgment."

I kept chipping away at her "guilt." Her lot was hard enough without her doing that to herself besides. "I just see, Amy, through all of this agony, how consistently you have wanted to do what is right. You've really poured yourself out for Bob. You still do as you visit him now and continue to oversee his care. I know you don't feel it, but I see how much you have loved him. The proof of love is actions much more than words or feelings."

"I guess that's been the hardest part of this. I don't feel any love at all. And Bob certainly doesn't think I love him. I can still take only so much over the phone. And every time I visit him, he turns it into a very unpleasant experience with his negative attitude. It wouldn't be so bad if I could bring him a special meal and we could enjoy it together, or wheel him outside in the garden and enjoy sitting and talking there, or play a game, or just have a decent conversation. But it's never that way. He doesn't want any of that. It's always just 'Where have you been?' and 'Why did you put me here?' and 'This, that, or something else is awful.' I leave feeling drained, and vowing I'll never go back again. But of course I do go back."

"He really takes all of his anger and frustration out on you, does-n't he? I hope you can see that it isn't mainly about you. It's about his whole condition."

"Sometimes I can see that, sometimes I can't."

I believe in meaningful sacrifice; I do not believe in meaningless sacrifice.[1] In Amy's case, meaningful sacrifice was all the care she lav-ished on Bob over the years, including seeing that he was as comfort-able as possible in the nursing home. Meaningful sacrifice was going to see him on a regular basis there, even though the encounter was unpleasant every time. Meaningless sacrifice would have been curtail-ing her own life and activity as Bob kept asking, because even that would not have been enough for him and it would have utterly killed her spirit. Meaningless sacrifice would have been visiting him as often as he wanted and as long, and leaving her phone open to his every call, because each encounter with him was a drain on her. I shared these thoughts with Amy. It is precisely this sort of specious spiritual good that constitutes good people's temptations.

How did I think about Bob? I felt immense compassion. If he had ever wanted to see me, I would have been glad to see him, and would probably have played a supportive role similar to the one I was playing with Amy. But from the beginning Bob had indicated that he didn't want to see any counselor, nor did he want to participate in any support group. I saw the mystery of his existence as hidden in the mystery of God, and it was mainly for him to work it out with God, as it is for each of us. We can help each other a little bit, but none of us can be God for anyone. One way to view Amy's periodic loss of perspective was that in those times she got her role confused and tried to be God for Bob— responsible for his condition, its meaning, his happiness. I frequently have to remind people in therapy that they are not God. And then I catch myself trying to be God as a therapist! It's quite a strain, I've dis-covered.

Choosing Life

Amidst the stress of her marital situation, which never seemed to abate, Amy, who was carrying a full-time job, returned to school for her doctorate. It was a decision she made herself, in the interest of improving herself and of eventually getting into the kind of work she really wanted to do. I supported her decision—with admiration—and I supported her on the journey; it was such a clear choice of life for herself. And that was precisely the point Amy stumbled over when she encountered adversity—which one does regularly in a doctoral program, especially at the dissertation stage.

"I feel so self-centered and self-absorbed as I pursue this whole project," she would say. "I turn on the answering machine so I can work uninterruptedly, and sometimes I don't return Bob's calls for hours. Maybe he's right. Maybe I'm selfish. I know he wants me up there for long visits on weekends, but I'd much rather be at home working on my dissertation."

I heard the voice of a woman who had finally found something she could really lose herself in. My heart rejoiced: God wants life for us! And in the background I heard the voice of her old friend, lacerating "guilt." There was more in the shadows here than Bob's refrain. So many women suffer from this. It is the sexist conditioning of a whole culture, and it is profoundly unjust. The conditioning tells women they should put others first, and that they should never get angry or "uppity." If a man were in Amy's position, tending a disabled wife, would he be battling "guilt" all the time if he also had a life of his own? I doubt it. A boy grows up thinking about what he wants to do in life, how he will establish his position in the world. If he chooses to marry, he will think of his family responsibility primarily in terms of supporting them by his work. He is not conditioned to put everybody else first, make sure everybody is happy—and then think of himself if there is anything left over. When Christian spirituality stresses service of others, women take it to heart and use it to reinforce their conditioning, while men for the most part don't hear it, or think they are already doing it.[2] Amy and I discussed selfishness, guilt, and conditioning many times over the years. She just about sabotaged herself out of the degree at the very end, when there was nothing left to do but put the finishing touches on her dissertation and get it in on time. All her "demons" rose up to defeat her at that moment, to put this consummate act of selfishness to death once and for all, and leave her right where she'd always been. It was a tremendous struggle. And she won.

Family of Origin Therapy

I had not seen Amy for months. I only knew that she had a new job and was enjoying it very much. She came back with the latest development.

"My mother died. As you know, she hadn't been well for some time. Still it was hard to lose her." Tears welled up.

"I went back east for the funeral. It wasn't an easy time. My siblings and I got into a big fight over funeral arrangements." She told me the details. "I came away devastated, and haven't heard from any of them since I'm home, several weeks now. It's probably all my fault. I've never been able to get along with them very well."

Amy set before me the story of her early years. As a child, she had not felt loved by either parent, nor by her siblings. Her father was not only distant but verbally abusive to her, frequently putting her down. Her mother seemed more critical than affectionate or affirming. The marriage was an unhappy one, the worst of it still residing in Amy's memory as scenes of her father's verbal and physical abuse of her mother. Amy had responded to the family's problems by trying to be the perfect child, hoping in this way finally to win love, as well as to create happier parents. It had become a life-script: she was still trying to be perfect, hoping at last to win some love and make everybody happy. But a few years ago, visiting her father in his last days, she found him still angry and abusive toward her mother and herself. Amy expressed a little of a lifetime's pent up anger, and her father effectively cursed her, telling her he never wanted to see her again. She returned to Seattle. Shortly thereafter her father died.

Now I understood better why Amy had so much trouble finishing her doctorate. To succeed or to be happy simply did not fit her script. She was supposed to be miserable, unloved and unsuccessful, because what she had internalized from her family experience was, "I am a 'bad person.' " Such long-standing convictions are hard to alter. But it seemed high time to do some family of origin therapy.

As Amy told me of the painful incidents she could remember, the verbal and nonverbal messages she had received, and the feelings she carried as a member of her family, I had her write some letters. These were letters she would never send, because her parents were dead and her siblings would probably not be able to respond in helpful ways.

The purpose of the writing was to allow Amy to speak from her heart about what hurt so much, and to tell it to those who had wronged her. Like many others, Amy had trouble with the assignment.

"I just can't criticize my parents. It's against all the rules."

"What rules? Family rules? Or moral and religious rules?"

"Both, actually. We were forbidden to express anger at home. We were told we had a bad attitude. I think religiously, too, I have real trouble writing a critical letter to my parents. I am supposed to honor and love them."

"But look what's at stake here—your healing. God wants life for you."

"I know that's the good news, but for me it's too good to be true."

"That's exactly the problem, Amy. You keep taking the blame for everything that happened. Getting healed consists essentially of being able to say to your parents, 'I was a neat kid, and you missed it. I deserved love, and you, for whatever reason, didn't know how to give it.' It's putting the responsibility back where it belongs."

"But I think I understand why they didn't love. Neither of them was loved much as a child either. My dad's dad was an alcoholic, and my mother's mother died when she was very young."

"That helps to explain it. But, you see, in this exercise you are not passing any ultimate judgment on your parents. That is for God to do. You are just looking critically as an adult at what they did and didn't do as parents—whatever the reasons or motives. There is nothing morally or spiritually wrong with that kind of assessment."

"I'm beginning to see what you're getting at."

"I think you'll probably feel some guilt as you do it. But it's false guilt, just like the false guilt you feel when you do something good for yourself. You'll have to bear with it for awhile. It will gradually fade."

With that, Amy was able to write the letters, and let the hurt and anger flow out. As we did this work, so late in our relationship, I asked myself if I should have led the way into this material years before. Amy had alluded to her family story on previous occasions. Perhaps I should have picked up on it. It was certainly clear now how germane her childhood was to everything she struggled with in the present. Yet it had always seemed to me she had come to me for a different purpose. She needed an "anchor," as she put it, to help her live with the constant burden of her ailing husband. It had never really occurred to me to shift the focus from that sustaining work. I don't know whether I was right or not.

The Awful Loneliness

Amy had spoken of her loneliness from time to time. It was certainly understandable.

"There is this huge ache inside me, a vast empty place nothing seems to fill. I seem to carry it with me everywhere. I don't think Bob and I were ever really married, even that year or so before he got sick. Neither of us was ready for marriage. And of course now, for years and years, we haven't been married at all. I have no one to lean on, no one to talk out the day's events with or to help shoulder the difficult decisions. But I think the hardest part is having no one to share the good things with, the experiences that cry out to be enjoyed with someone."

I could easily empathize. There is a measure of loneliness, it seems, in every human being. I think it has spiritual significance, and I wondered if Amy had thought about that.

"What you are saying really makes sense, Amy. I can hear what an ache it has been. What I'm wondering is, do you think your loneliness could have any deeper meaning?"

"What do you mean?"

"Well, when you think of the ultimate meaning of your life, what significance might your loneliness have?"

She thought a minute. "Maybe it's about God," she said. Maybe it's my longing for God even more than for a husband."

I nodded and smiled. If we are made for union with God, it would be reasonable to expect that hunger to show up somewhere in our experience.

"Any other significance you can think of?"

"What is this, twenty questions? Well, it probably means I'm supposed to reach out to other people, too. Maybe I don't do that enough."

"You're good at this. I should come to you for counseling." Really though, she had articulated two important insights. Starting with the longing for a mate, she had expanded her awareness to recognize the longing for God and for other people hidden inside it.

"And that's basic Christian spirituality, isn't it?" "I said. In the gospels, Jesus goes off to lonely places to pray, and he involves himself with people at every turn. He shows us what we are made for. And what he models, he also preaches."

"I remember one night when I was teaching in Korea as a Jesuit," I went on. "I was feeling extremely lonely. I was unmarried, and living in a foreign country. In my need, I went to the room of my closest friend, but he wasn't there. I went to the room of my next closest friend, and he wasn't there either. Filled with heartache, I went up to the roof of the building we lived in. It was flat, and I sometimes went there to pray. I walked back and forth in my loneliness that night, my heart crying to God. What amazed me was that God comforted me, directly. It was totally unexpected and wonderful. I went back in feeling much better, glad my two friends had not been in their rooms."

She was listening intently, apparently trying this idea on. "I know I don't do that often enough."

"I don't either. And I'm not saying God comforts me every time I feel lonely. I just mean I learned that night how we carry around a big empty sanctuary inside waiting to be filled by God. It's built in."

I wanted to push the social side of the equation, too, because I knew Amy kept to herself a lot, mostly out of a sense that she had nothing to offer. What a lie that was.

"How are you doing for friends, Amy?"

"Not too well. I do have some solid women friends who have stuck by me no matter what. But I have to admit that I hold back a lot in relationships. It is hard for me to trust. And I don't want to be a burden."

"When you say you don't want to be a burden, you're thinking about your husband, right?" She nodded. "You don't want to be always talking about your problem, which is always on your mind, right?" She nodded. "I think you're making a mistake. First, it's quite all right to talk to your friends from time to time about Bob. They would find it very strange if you did not. And women are wonderful at supporting one another with things like that. But it also seems you are defining yourself way too narrowly: 'I am the woman with the ailing husband.' There is so much more to you than that, Amy. You are intelligent. You are accomplished. You're funny. You're reading all the time. You are warm, and curious about other people and about many things. You have a doctorate and a very rich work experience. *All* of that is what you are. Your 'problem' is indeed large, but it is just one corner of your personal reality."

"You really make 'my personal reality' sound like something."

"It *is* something. You are the only one who doesn't know it. Again, the childhood residue shows itself here: 'I am nobody and nothing.' Whereas in fact you have developed a very rich personhood, and many people would be delighted to have someone like you for a friend."

I could see I was battling a fair bit of incredulity here. But if she could begin to believe me, who knew her so well, she could perhaps begin to hear and believe the same message when it was spoken by others, as I was sure it already was. It is amazing how much love and affirmation we are given which we simply let fall to the ground.

To help her gradually get over her difficulty in trusting, I suggested she choose someone in her present circle of acquaintances who seemed relatively safe, likelier than the others to be respectful, gentle, and capable of confidences. I proposed that she start letting herself out to that person a little bit at a time, beginning with fairly small things, testing each time to see how it went. She could stop at any point she wanted. That way, without venturing too much or really losing anything, she would gradually be building closeness, and becoming more comfortable with it. It might lead to a deep friendship. She agreed to try it.

There is another thing I like to do with loneliness, or with any bad feeling someone is trying to keep at bay. That is to invite the person to befriend it, to draw it in closer and feel and explore it.[3] I asked Amy if she was game, and she was, so I had her close her eyes and relax. Then I invited her to let her loneliness surface, and just to be with it, fully attentive. What did it feel like emotionally? What were the physical sensations that went with it? Were there any images it presented? Letting all this happen takes courage. It is exactly what we usually avoid, fearing it might overwhelm us. With a supportive person present and some encouragement, it becomes a little less forbidding.

The direction the exercise took with Amy was a sort of waking dream, rich in imagery. Her loneliness presented itself as a huge, dark, empty gymnasium in which she sat desolate. But as she stayed with it, light began streaming in from the top. Then a door appeared in the wall, and she walked out into a world of people she knew, who invited her to join in their activities. This experience, which created itself, perfectly replicated in symbol what we had talked about—how our loneliness is our heart's cry for God and for other people, toward whom we must reach out. Amy felt comforted by the exercise, and I suggested she put it in writing or sketches for herself. We tried the exercise again the next session, and again a waking dream unfolded, but with entirely different imagery. This time Amy found herself alone on the beach, bucking strong winds with waves crashing around her. She struggled to a grassy plateau where she found children and played with them. The weather turned calm and sunny. Then the children invited her to jump over a kind of chasm with them, but she was afraid and was left behind. The fog rolled in. Seeing her predicament, I suggested she ask Jesus to come. He came. She felt loved. He helped her across the chasm, and she played some more with him and the children. Again she felt comforted by the experience. Again I suggested she write it up or sketch it.

After these sessions, Amy no longer felt so much the victim of her loneliness. She had embraced and integrated it more into her selfhood, rather than trying to stave it off. It did not frighten her so much anymore. And she had experienced some possibilities in it, where before it had just seemed barren. Like the body, the psyche carries within itself the instruments of its own healing. All it needs is some facilitation.

The Quiet Transformation

I did not see it coming. Amy herself did not realize it was happening. We had been talking about Bob for years, and I began to notice a difference. I spoke of it first.

"Amy, are you aware that something has changed inside you?"

"What do you mean?"

"I don't think you're angry anymore." She looked at me, surprised. "When you talk about Bob now, there is a whole different tone. It seems that compassion is now the deepest of all your feelings about Bob."

"I guess I wasn't fully aware of it, but yes, I do really feel for him now. He just keeps going down. He can no longer turn himself in bed, or hold up his head in his wheelchair. His breathing is labored now, and he has to struggle to form each word. Most people can't understand what he's saying. He is totally dependent for every small-est thing he needs. It hurts me." Tears came, which did not happen easily with Amy.

"This whole long saga of yours reminds me of a letter I just got from a priest friend of mine who ministers with the Indian people on a reservation in South Dakota. All around him are broken families, alcoholism, poverty, abuse, suicide, bleak prospects, and all of it is years and years old. What he wrote was, 'I feel as if I am standing at the foot of the cross. Above me hangs Jesus in his agony. And there isn't a thing I can do to take him down. Yet I feel I belong here.' "

We were silent.

Amy had always acknowledged that Bob had an extremely diffi-cult life, and had felt sorry for him. But the implications for her had dominated her emotional and practical life, eclipsing her compassion. Now that had shifted, and I could only marvel.

"It is grace," I said.

"Yes, it is grace."

"Something from somewhere, unexpected, transforming, making the impossible somehow possible."

"Yes. I pray that Bob will die. But it is not mainly for me. I pray for his release from his dreadful imprisonment, for his homecoming and his peace."

"So do I. I pray for your release too. I've been wondering, Amy. Has Bob's attitude changed at all?"

"Not that I can see. But it doesn't get to me so much anymore. I just wish there was something I could do for him." Again her sadness was profound. I just sat, sharing it with her.

And her vigil with Bob continued.

Amy was a more peaceful person now. And she had let herself get closer to me. Neither change had come easily, but only bit by bit over many years. From her childhood rejection and isolation, Amy had learned a self-reliance and self-sufficiency that made it very difficult for her to be weak with anyone or ask for anything. She had come to me for help, I think, because she simply could not carry her burden alone anymore, try though she had. She allowed herself to make some demands on me only because she was paying for it. But this too had softened over time, along with her anger. She could be vulnerable now; she could open up. She could let herself depend a little. She could care too. It was different to be with her now—easier, warmer, more tranquil. Had I changed too, contributing to this newness? I hope so.

****

Should my work with Amy be called therapy or spiritual direction? I think it could appropriately be called either, because it is both. What I essentially did for her is the sort of companioning a therapist often does over a long period of time with some clients, serving as the person to whom they unfold and from whom they receive mainly emotional support, some feedback, occasional suggestions. But spiritual directors, if they do not insist on too narrow a focus, do much the same thing for those who visit them: listen to them talk about their lives, support and encourage them, love them, and offer them occasional suggestions. The difference is that spiritual direction takes place in the context of a mutually shared faith vision, where therapy might not. For me, the healing purpose and the faith vision coalesce, so that I see myself as always doing both therapy and spiritual direction. That is how I view my work with Amy.

The mystery of Amy's life is hidden in God, bound up with a husband who cannot be a husband but is instead a heavy responsibility to her, with the family she came from and the strengths and weaknesses she derived from it, with the struggles and rewards of her work and her friends, with the therapist she has asked to walk along. It is in all of that that she engages God, for God is where the action is in her life—working with her for her growth and her good. I cannot begin to explain the mystery of it all. But I believe it is a benevolent mystery, and part of my role is to share that belief as hope, and foster its working.

9.

Who Am I—Really?

This is my own story—an important chapter of it anyway. It is the account of how I was sailing along and came to a crisis, a major turning point in my life. I sought help from a clinical psychologist, who was also a Jesuit priest. So this chapter too is a story of therapy and spiritual direction, but this time I'm on the receiving end.

The Background

I was raised in a "good Catholic family," the seventh of nine children. We went to church as a family every Sunday, confessed our sins to the priest at least once a month (even during the summer), and said the family rosary every evening after dinner before anybody could move. When the family was in any trouble, we made novenas, a method of "storming heaven" by saying the same set of prayers nine times at regular intervals, usually once a day but sometimes once every hour, depending on how fast we needed help. I do not know where that method of approaching God originated, but I'm sure it has a venerable tradition. In the hallway of our home we had a little shrine to the Sacred Heart of Jesus with a vigil light always burning before it. In May we put the Sacred Heart in temporary storage because May was the Blessed Mother's month, and she got the shrine and the vigil light along with flowers. We went to Mother of Perpetual Help devotions at church on Tuesdays once a month, devotions before the Blessed Sacrament on Fridays once a month, and the annual Novena of Grace—nine straight nights at church repeating the same prayers to St. Ignatius Loyola and St. Francis Xavier, and listening, of course, to lengthy sermons. Over the mantel in our living room hung a large painting of Christ crowned with thorns. What impression that made on visitors at large they had the delicacy never to say, but I know it slowed down my sisters' boyfriends in their amorous advances. That, and my Mom or Dad turning the porchlight on and off several times in quick succession when one of my sisters and her boyfriend sat out in the car after a date, helped us honor chastity, the cornerstone of the

Catholic faith. Since we were a large family with but one breadwinner, we kept a statue of St. Joseph with a dime under it in a nook in the kitchen next to where the rosaries hung. St. Joseph was in charge of our financial affairs. Whenever my parents fell seriously afoul of one another, which happened from time to time, it was the parish priest to whom they had recourse (therapists were for crazy people), and we had a large number of priests who were friends over for dinner all through the years. My parents sacrificed a lot to send us all to good Catholic schools, where we were taught by nuns and priests the first twelve years of our academic lives. There, daily mass was *de rigeur*.

It will come as no surprise that when it came time to choose careers, not a few of us chose religious life and priesthood. Four of the six girls, and all three of the boys, headed for convent and seminary. I do not know if this was part of my parents' conscious (or unconscious) plan, but judging from the number of pictures they took of us in our black and white outfits, they seemed to feel proud. Religious progeny were grand slam homers in the Catholic ghetto we grew up in. And legend had it that for a Catholic mother, having a priest son was an automatic ticket to heaven. My memory is dim as to whether the father got in on that deal or not.

I entered the Jesuits right after high school. The Jesuits ran the best boys' high school in Milwaukee, and besides being religious our family had aspirations to be the best. Religious life had the nicest way of reinforcing everything that in generous measure I already was: bright, highly disciplined, sexually repressed, idealistic, responsible for others, loyal, determined to excel. Jesuit life is life lived in all-male communities organized around the vows of perpetual poverty, chastity, and obedience. Like other priests and religious women and men, Jesuits are dedicated to the service of others for the sake of God's kingdom. The specific work of the Jesuits within the larger context of the church's mission is the intellectual life. Rather than doing parish work, Jesuits are chiefly teachers, running high schools and universities and doing research and writing, all with a view to bringing the gospel to bear on the intellectual and cultural life of the world.

Jesuit community was my life context from ages 18–31, when I was at last ordained a priest. By that time I had two masters' degrees, and I would go on to get a Ph.D. It was a life of work and prayer. And while I did not particularly like living in all-male communities (I am not a community-type person, and I like women at least as well as men), I had some wonderful individual men friends and we shared our lives in depth. I loved the years of study, and I loved priestly work. I did well at both and was highly regarded by my peers and those I ministered to by teaching, counseling, and administering the seven sacraments of the Roman Catholic tradition. The toughest part of the life for me was chastity. Like many young men, I did not enter seminary because I did not wish to marry. I went because I thought God wanted me to, and I understood marriage to be the sacrifice God was asking of me. It did not go down easy. My hormones ran ably. And I found women warm and wonderful, starting with my own sisters.

The Crisis

A strange thing happened just three months after I was ordained at 31. I went to Berkeley to do doctoral studies in theology. My assignment was to get a Ph.D. and take it to Sogang Jesuit University in Seoul, Korea, there to spend the rest of my life. I had already spent three years teaching in Korea, learned the daunting language, and mingled well with the people. The university needed theologians, and I was a logical choice. So I settled in Berkeley to get the Ph.D., and one of the first people I met was a nun from Portland by the name of Kathy who had just arrived for the same purpose. I liked her right away.

We took some of the same courses. We went to some of the same liturgies. We came together in group social activities, and participated in the same discussion clubs. Our friendship just would not stop growing. Deeper feelings emerged. After about two years we realized we were in love. That was simply not in the plans, either ours or, as we understood them, God's, yet there it was. All of our efforts went into containing the friendship within the narrow boundaries of our commitments. After four years in Berkeley, both of us had our Ph.D.s and we parted company for distant places, she for Portland, I for St. Louis, both to do university teaching. It was a dreadful parting, but it seemed the only thing to do.

During my last year in Berkeley, I had reached a decision not to return to Korea. A growing feeling deep inside, a kind of dread, told me I would never make it as a celibate in that context. I was already being talked about as next president of the university, mission superior, or both. I knew from my experience how lonely it was living with the uncongeniality and privations of a foreign culture, and I was sure it was even lonelier at the top. The founder of the mission, a priest I greatly respected, had ended by marrying one of our students, at least 20 years his junior. At the time, it was a major scandal. Others had left the community, returned to the States and married. Knowing the personal cost of celibacy, yet convinced I was to live out my life as a celibate priest, I took a step to make it a little more possible, asking for work in the States rather than abroad. And so I was assigned to St. Louis University, to teach full-time and to be Superior to a small community of young Jesuits in formation.

Kathy and I did not see each other at all that year, but I can tell you that I thought about her. After that year, I was reassigned to Berkeley, where there was a huge community of Jesuits in studies. I was Vice-Rector, professor, and spiritual director to many of the men in theological studies just prior to their ordination. It all kept me extremely busy, but it did little to lessen an abiding ache for Kathy. She was still in Portland teaching theology. We met a couple of times in the next two years when a theology conference would bring her to the Bay area, or a retreat would take me to the Northwest. Such days were easily the happiest of my life. They stood out the way Mount Rainier towers over the Cascade range. Our love seemed to grow when we were together, and grow some more when we were apart. We were apart almost all the time. It was an agony.

By this time, I had been a Jesuit for twenty years. Every time I raised the celibacy question with my spiritual directors, Jesuits of high quality whom I loved and who loved me, I got the same response: "I know what you mean, Tom. We all feel that desire to marry from time to time. You have these deep feelings because you are such a warm and healthy human being. That's exactly why you are such a fine priest. Look at all the good you are doing. Everybody has tremendous respect for you." That is all it took to reinforce my own thriving superego, which was capable enough unassisted most of the time. Remember my conditioning. So down went my sexuality again, into its cage in my psyche. But how it roared.

Then a strange and wonderful thing happened. There lived in

Santa Barbara a Jesuit priest who was also a clinical psychologist, much esteemed as a spiritual director, assigned to forming young Jesuits, and several times chosen as Superior of communities. He was ten years my senior. Our paths had crossed several times in California, and we enjoyed each other's company. One night we went out to dinner together, in the spring of the seventh year of my friendship with Kathy, and at the end of a very enjoyable evening as I was dropping him off, I remarked: "You know, Leo, I love being a priest. I don't even mind working six and a half days a week. I would just like someone to come home to." And with one line he blew my mind.

"That doesn't seem like too much to ask," he said simply.

That response was so different from any I had ever received on this topic that it took up residence and stayed for weeks right in the center of my mind. It finally freed up the question I had been pushing down so hard for so many years: "What did I really want to do with the rest of my life?" I was forty years old.

There was only one way I could think of that question: What was God's will in the matter? That is what I had to do. On any other platform, my life could make no sense to me. And of course it had seemed to me ever since I was a boy that God's will for me was to be a priest. I had publicly and solemnly vowed it for life. So the question now was, could it possibly be God's will that I marry? In the Roman church, priesthood and marriage are mutually exclusive.

I approached Leo and asked him if I could make the thirty-day retreat under his guidance, and see him regularly during the next year for spiritual direction. He graciously agreed, and we had many conversations over the next year. Here commences the most intensive therapy and spiritual direction of my life. Here the road bends. I will try to capture the gist of our conversations in the following pages.

What Is God's Will for Me?

"Here's my dilemma, Leo. I feel called to be a priest. People tell me I'm a good priest. But I am also deeply in love with an extraordinary woman. We've tried to keep that love within the framework of our commitments. But it is growing just too big. We feel we've got to make a choice. What the question comes down to for me personally is: What does God want me to do? That is what I've got to figure out."

It would be interesting to me to know how a therapist who did not share my spiritual framework would have worked with me on that question. Here is how Leo responded.

"Tom, the real question is, What do *you* most deeply want to do? That may sound strange to you. But when you have found what you most deeply want, you will have found God's will for you."

"Wait a minute. I don't see that what I want has anything to do with it. It is what God wants that is important. Doesn't the gospel tell me to die to myself and embrace the cross?"

"We are called to die to our false selves, never to our true self. Our true self is what God wants us most fully to be. Surely God the creator and God the redeemer are not opposed to one another. The God who made your inner being wants that core to unfold and develop. How could Jesus contradict that? That is what I mean when I say when you find your own deepest wanting, your own true energy and orientation, you have found God's leading in your life. God's will for each of us is enfolded in our inner being, where it keeps revealing itself to us."

"That just sounds too easy, Leo. I'd love to be married to Kathy. But I feel called to be a priest."

"That's a hard choice. Which do you really want? When I say 'deepest level of wanting' I don't mean a whim or a fancy. I mean the mature product of your feeling and your thinking. It takes time to crystallize. I don't mean any 'should' either, which always comes from outside yourself. Parents, society, church fill our heads with 'shoulds.' As we mature, we sort through all the values represented by those shoulds, deciding which ones are true values for ourselves. Your choices have to come out of your own *owned* values. Those have been integrated right into your being. You live from them. You feel them here," he said, putting his hand over his stomach, "not here," he said, pointing to his head.

I had to walk around with that idea awhile. I could hardly believe what a difference it made in the way I thought about God. More than thought, it was a deep down feeling that stirred refreshingly. Could God really be that good? Does God give us that much freedom? Does God genuinely want me to be happy—not just to labor for the kingdom? I had always believed God was good and wanted what was good for me. But I thought God was very demanding too. Hadn't God required Abraham to sacrifice his only son Isaac?[1] In my view, it was typical of God to ask the harder thing. I had been schooled to believe that for the spiritual person the congenial course was probably the wrong course. Could it be true that God wanted me to have what I wanted, that Kathy might be God's *gift* to me, not a terrible temptation sent to purify me? What a thought. That was a God I could love, not just serve.

But sorting out what I really wanted presented its own difficulties. Now I was caught between two great loves: my priesthood and Kathy. By legislation of the Roman Catholic Church at the Fourth Lateran Council in 1154, being a priest *and* married was no longer possible. It was one or the other. I had to choose.

"I see now that God's will lives within my own deepest wanting. My question now, Leo, is, how do I figure out what I really want?"

"It may take a little time to crystallize. It's not something to figure out. In major matters, your whole being tells you. You feel it deep inside. Let me put the question about your deepest wanting in a couple of other ways, to help you get at it. What brings you to life? In what circumstances do you feel most alive, most fully yourself? What stirs your enthusiasm and energy? What option gives you a feeling of rightness? That is what you are trying to get in touch with."

"Even as you say it, Leo, it's clear to me that it is living my life with Kathy. What you are describing is how I feel when I am with her—and I'm not talking about the first flush of being in love. We've been close friends for seven years now. There is this immense vitality that surges up in me when I am with her; usually it feels trapped inside. When we are apart, both the vitality and the joy are greatly diminished."

"There you are. That is what I mean."

"I've got to sit with this awhile though, Leo. This is all brand new. I've got to sit with priesthood too, because I love being a priest, and it is very hard for me to think of giving it up."

The Question of Fidelity

So I sat, and walked, and prayed. Always the thought of Kathy brought deep joy. The thought of priesthood brought various feelings. Priesthood began to separate out into two parts: the ministry itself, and the life-style. It was the ministry I loved, the working with and for people. The life-style, in all-male community settings, felt constricted and barren to me. But even that had to be considered closely. My fellow Jesuits were good men, and some were close friends. I had committed myself to this group, and we shared a mission that gave profound meaning to our lives. My role models were there. And I myself had become a role model for others, the younger Jesuits I taught and had in spiritual direction, all the people outside the community I had taught, preached to, counseled, given retreats to, corresponded with. They looked up to me, depended on me somehow. What effect would my leaving to marry have on all these people?

"Leo, we've got to talk about fidelity. What about commitment? What about responsibility? They've always been important values to me. What about vows?"

"Fidelity is certainly an important issue. But the question is, fidelity to what? We have to be very careful about that. When you took your vows, what were you trying to say? You were committing yourself to God and to God's work, to living the gospel as fully as you could, right? Of course, you did it within a particular historical structure, Jesuit community, because at the time it seemed to you the best setting for living out that fundamental commitment. To what must you be faithful? Historical structures keep changing. So does your own unfolding personal truth. The values abide. The question we have to keep asking ourselves is, How do I keep living out my values now? How do I remain true to myself now? These are what I must be faithful to."

"But what effect will my leaving have on people?"

"That's putting the cart before the horse. What effect will your leaving or staying have on *you*? That is what you are really responsible for. Other people are responsible for themselves."

"But isn't that selfish?"

"Tom, what if you gain the whole world, but lose your own soul, your own *self*?" (Mk 8:35)

That saying of Jesus was very familiar. But I had always thought it reared itself against the foolishness of putting all your efforts in this life into becoming rich, famous, powerful—only to find yourself in hell in the next. My mentor was putting quite a new spin on it. He was talking true self [2] again, and asserting that without it we are nothing, whatever else we might count to our credit.

"Tom, have you ever looked around our communities at the older retired men?" I certainly had. "What do you see?"

"I'm afraid in too many cases I see bitter, angry old men. I don't mean all, by any means. Some are still fresh, young at heart, happy. But too many seem loveless, joyless, simply unemployable anywhere."

"That's another way of coming at the question—by the fruits of various kinds of fidelity. Those men have supposedly been 'faithful.' But faithful to what? To the rule, perhaps. To whatever their superiors told them to do, perhaps. To the letter of a promise they made when they were young, perhaps. Is that true fidelity, true responsibility? What about faithfulness to oneself, to the unfolding truth of one's being, to genuine, abiding value?"

I can always tell when I am hearing the truth. Something moves deep within me. This was a far more exciting—and freeing—vision of fidelity than any I had ever heard before. And so I sat with the fidelity issue awhile, trying to assimilate and apply to my own case the insight I had gained.

Scandal

But I was still worried about all those people for whom I was a priest. And I was more than a little frightened about what kind of work I might end up doing if I left. I didn't want to give up my priestly ministry. Not only did it seem to be from God. It was me. Being some kind of a salesman or businessman or administrator seemed a dreadful prospect. That was another day's conversation.

"I realize I am mainly responsible for myself, not for other people. But I do worry about what kind of effect my leaving will have on others."

"Those who love you will continue to love you no matter what you do. After all, you will still be the same person. Those who 'love' you just because you are a priest, well, what kind of love is that? And how much does the opinion of those people matter to you? As far as the issue of 'scandal' is concerned, each of us has to follow our own truth whether other people understand and support it or not. And people's faith? It is rooted in something more solid and dependable than what you or I happen to do with our lives—or it ought to be. Your leaving might actually help a few people get their faith more properly rooted. But the larger number, I suspect, will not be affected at that level at all. There is also the possibility that your finding yourself might help some others find themselves. But again, these are not the matters your decision really hinges on."

"I guess part of what I'm worried about is what I'll do if I leave. Selling cars or computers would be just as ill-fitting and uncomfortable a suit of clothes for me as celibacy has been. I would slowly die inside. That in itself sometimes seems a sufficient reason to stay put. I have all this training and these gifts, and I want to keep using them for other people."

"Of course. That's your call, isn't it—priesthood in some form? That has persisted in you through all this prayer and dialogue, and through all the years. But, Tom, look at the world. There are needs everywhere. There is no way we can begin to meet them all. Jesuits meet a few of them, in a few places. Many other people of every kind meet others of them. As for you, whether you are here or someplace else, a Jesuit priest or something else, you will be needed and you will respond. I don't think you have to worry at all, with your dedication and talent, that you will not be able to find a way. And who is to say that you will do any less good there than you have done here? Maybe you'll do more."

"I love the breadth of your vision, Leo. And what you are saying is true to my experience. I've worked in Seoul, St. Louis, Berkeley, and other places. In each place, the needs seemed so great that I felt indispensable, and people tried to keep me there. But as soon as I'd go someplace else, the needs there were so absorbing that the previous place would soon fade. And I'd always learn subsequently that life went on in all those places quite well without me! If I leave the Jesuit context and the priesthood as I have known it, I've got to find another way to keep doing the sorts of things I've been doing. But you know what really hurts, Leo? That I can't be married and be a priest. Why should I have to choose between these two great loves of mine when they are perfectly compatible?"

He shook his head sadly. "That's one of the great tragedies of our time. The Catholic priesthood is losing—just wasting—countless high-quality individuals like yourself over this crazy piece of human legislation binding celibacy to priesthood. I'm really sorry you can't do both. It's got to change, and eventually it will. Meanwhile...."

Meanwhile I sat, and walked, and prayed over my choice. Some days I had a feeling of rightness or peace about leaving and marrying. Other days I found myself more at home in the option of remaining where I was, saying goodby to the whole gamble of marriage and new work. I told Leo of this vacillating back and forth. I was afraid I might never be able to make up my mind.

"Sounds like you're not ready to decide," he said simply. "Give it time." I loved his respect for nature. His response implied hope: I would not remain on the fence forever.

Freedom

I had an instructive experience while making the 30-day retreat during the nine months Leo and I spent together. The retreat, based on the *Spiritual Exercises* of St. Ignatius, is divided into four "weeks," the length of each week variable according to what is happening to the retreatant. When the director determines that the retreatant has completed one of the weeks, he or she gives the retreatant a break day before beginning the next part. I was in the 17th or 18th day when I woke up one morning with no taste for retreating whatsoever. But it was not the time for a break day. I went to see Leo that morning as usual to inform him of what I was experiencing and receive guidance for the day.

"Leo, I should probably just mention that I don't feel like it at all today. I'd rather be doing almost anything else." I said this simply to inform him. I fully expected to go through the day as usual. In fact, I was sure he would say it was especially important that I be scrupulously faithful to the schedule of the retreat that day because it was at just such times of desolation that retreatants derive the most profit.

"Sounds as if you need a break," he said simply. "Why don't you take the day off? You can do anything you feel like. Let me see, there's a car free, so you're certainly welcome to that, if you'd like."

I sat there stunned. Suddenly given my freedom, I didn't know whether I wanted to take it or not. "That's not exactly the answer I was expecting," I said. "Let me go off and think about it awhile. I'll tell you what I come up with. Thanks for the offer of the car."

Thirty minutes later I was back at his door. "This will probably surprise you, but I've decided I want to stay in retreat today. I just want to pray one hour less. I'm feeling good again. Thanks a lot. See you tomorrow morning."

And I had a most enjoyable day, thoroughly peaceful with what I was doing. On that morning, I had learned the difference between a *should* and a *want*, and I would never forget it. They may cover exactly the same territory—in this case, a retreat day—but the feelings are a world apart. I feel my shoulds in my head, with constraint or tightness. I feel my wants in my belly, with expansion and energy. Leo had said on a previous occasion that "wholehearted wanting is the only sound basis of motivation." I enjoyed my day because I was doing what I wanted. It was exactly the same agenda I had dreaded when it felt imposed—solitude, silence, prayer, reading, walking, eucharist—with one small exception, four instead of five hours of formal prayer. When Leo gave me my freedom, I walked out of that agenda and then right back into it, but with a completely different feeling. It was where I freely chose to be. It was a small analogy with the way he was guiding me in the larger matter of my priesthood.

The rest is history. Over the months I came more and more to a solid feeling of rightness about leaving the Jesuits and marrying, to carry on my priesthood in a new way. Meanwhile, in a distant city, Kathy had gone through her own equally adventuresome discernment process, and reached a similar decision.

When I shared with Leo what I had arrived at, he volunteered two remarks that touched me deeply.

"Tom, somehow by the choice you are freely making, I feel confirmed in the choice I freely make. I can't fully explain how. But I choose to stay here, and I'm happy in that choice." Leo was a marvelously free man, and he invited others to freedom. St. Paul himself extols "the freedom of the children of God" (Rm 8:21; see also Gal 4:1–7), but we keep forgetting that freedom is God's gift to us.

The second thing he said was: "Tom, you will always be my brother priest." Wow! So many good men have "left" to marry, thoroughly shamed by their former brothers for having been weak, unfaithful, and lacking the fortitude to do the right thing. Here was a priest I greatly respected telling me I was still what he was. Part of

Leo's freedom consisted precisely in resisting the tight categories within which so many others are bound.[3]

It is fifteen years later. I am happily married to Kathy. I am a full-time therapist, a part-time theology professor, and a writer in the fields of theology and therapy. My wife, likewise a theologian and a therapist, engages in the same three professional activities. In fact, we've written four books together, besides the four each of us has written separately. We look upon all that we do as ministry, though we no longer enjoy any official status in our church. Our marriage has greatly enriched my priesthood. Hers, too, I think, though the Roman church has not formally ordained any women for a good many centuries. Our relationship has made better persons of both of us. One can hardly fail to be enriched by a special love. Nor can one fail to be refined in the crucible of intimacy.

As I look back on the time I spent with Leo, I see how what we both called spiritual direction was also therapy through and through. He too thinks of the two as very closely allied. Our work together was all under the aegis of my finding God's will for my life. But I experienced a deep healing and a wonderful liberation in the process. Is that not precisely what therapy seeks to bring about? Leo helped me find my *self*, and to live more authentically from the core of my being. That sounds like therapy too. He assisted me in making a decision that was consistent with my most cherished beliefs and values, even though it involved a fresh and surprising departure. He supported me through a transition that was fraught with peril, from which I could easily have emerged damaged, riddled with "guilt" and a loss of personal identity. With his help I came out instead solidly on my feet, seeing clearly and feeling good about myself. The therapy I needed could only have taken place within the spiritual framework in which my whole life was grounded. With great skill, Leo led me into new experiences of freedom and selfhood, and into the presence and activity of God in those profoundly personal realms. It was a therapeutic/spiritual adventure in personal integration.[4]

I shared my draft of this chapter with Leo, to give him an opportunity to change anything he remembered differently or felt uncomfortable with my publishing. He wrote this reply:

"I have read your recollection of our conversations. They match mine. I was deeply moved as I read your words. And they confirm what I believe. Here is how I would say it. When we are born we are given clear title of ownership over that piece of property which is our self. But long before we can exercise the rights of this God-given ownership, all kinds of liens and rights-of-way cloud that title. And there are others—family, church, state, individuals— who claim to have bought and paid for shares in the property. Human growth is clearing title to the property. Isn't this the goal of that process called variously spiritual direction and therapy? Clearing title so that self-possession is possible. We can share, we can give, only what we possess. To me this seems self-evident."

When Kathy and I got married, a Protestant minister friend remarked: "I can't quite put it together in my mind. In your church this is a 'scandal.' In ours, it would be cause for great rejoicing—that two such people had found one another and joined their lives and ministries. It seems to me like a great gift of God, to you two and to everybody else as well."

Yes! Hidden Spring.

Part Three

FURTHER QUESTIONS

10.

Questions about Practice

As you have read these chapters, questions have undoubtedly arisen in your mind. Let me close by answering the ones I am most commonly asked.

1. How much do you talk about God in therapy?

In the total scheme of things, not all that much. During most sessions I do not find occasion to talk about God. The spiritual dimension is the matrix within which "we live and move and have our being," as Paul says (Acts 17); it is the foundation of everything. And so in therapy it is the larger framework within which we are working on the client's problem or concern. It gives us our ultimate values, our general orientation, and our deepest energy. But once the issue under discussion has been placed in this spiritual perspective, there is not usually a great deal more to be said in that regard. Most of the time goes into exploring the problem or concern, expressing feelings, interpreting experience, looking at options, providing support, developing strategies, reporting on progress and failure and problems remaining, putting matters in different perspectives, working toward solution or acceptance. God seems to expect us to work with our own wits and resources, and in most therapy sessions that is where the time and energy go. Yet all these activities take on a different significance when the therapist and client approach the session from a spiritual perspective.

I do not remember any client who has ever said to me, "You talk about God too much. Let's get practical." Or, "Don't lay that religious stuff on me; I'm not the religious type." The opposite has happened to me more often—though still not very often. "I thought you dealt explicitly with the spiritual dimension. I don't hear you saying much about it."

This kind of feedback has always brought me up short, making me realize that I am assuming something and not talking enough about it. I am assuming that we share a common spiritual field, and that its implications for what we are discussing are obvious. Or I am assuming they know that all of my responses to practical questions come out of a vision of faith even if I do not mention it.

In this regard, the story chapters above might be misleading. They sound as if in doing therapy we talk mainly about the spiritual dimension, and that I offer lengthy disquisitions on it. If I did, I doubt that I would have any clients! Actually, most of the time we work very practically on the client's presenting problems. The stories are recounted as they are precisely to highlight the spiritual dimension.

2. Can you summarize the ways you typically work with the spiritual dimension in therapy?

First, I try to be with and for people in the manner I think God is with and for them—genuinely interested, respectful, compassionate, accepting, hopeful, affirming yet also challenging. I believe that God is at work in me when I relate to others in this spirit. I also believe that God is already present and active in the client's life, and that God is particularly active with them in the crisis that brings them to therapy.

Then, I affirm or confirm all that I see in them that shows the spiritual life they are living. People tend to be underaware of their own goodness and harmony with God's values and purposes. So I name the gifts I see that God has given them, the good (spiritual) choices they are making, the special graces which I observe coming to them as we go along, whether in the form of a fresh insight, a new strength, a liberation, or an inner transformation. Usually, the more we are aware that God is with us, the happier we feel and the more inclined we are to be even more aware of and responsive to God.

Regularly, after I hear about a whole situation with which a client is struggling, I ask the question: "Where do you think God is in all this?" I want to get them thinking about this in case they are not, because I think the spiritual dimension is so helpful. And I want to approach the matter collaboratively, with both of us sharing the insights we get.[1] The first answer the client gives to this question is often less cogent than the answers that unfold over time as the client continues to ruminate simply because such a question has been asked.

I will articulate a spiritual principle I feel is relevant to a given situation. It is usually one of the ten I name in chapter 3, or one that comes out of the faith vision presented in chapter 1, e.g., "God is the depth dimension of all your experience." Usually I elaborate a little, and make sure the client understands.

I sometimes challenge a client's beliefs. I challenge a belief which shows itself to be operative in the person's life when I see that that belief is hurting rather than helping the cause of life, and that it is of questionable validity. An example is the belief that whenever I take anything for myself, I am guilty of selfishness. Or the belief that God mainly sees my sinfulness and so stands over me habitually as a judgmental, disapproving presence. Or the belief that what I want and what God wants can be presumed to be opposed. Or the belief that any particular religious injunction is more important than the commandment to love ourselves and others. In challenging such beliefs, I might simply state what I believe and why. Or I might put the challenge in the form of a question: "Do you really believe God wants you to be miserable the rest of your life?" Or, "If you really loved someone, would you make the demand (or judgment) of that person that you seem to think God is making of you?" Or, "Why do you believe that?"

Finally, I remind people of truths I know they hold but are forgetting. Chief among these is that God is with and for them where they are in their lives right now, as they are, and in whatever suffering or struggle they are experiencing. And, of course, that in all things God is working with them for good, whether we can see how right now or not. These truths are always comforting and sustaining, and all of us need to be reminded of them when, typically in difficulty, we forget.

3. How do you deal with someone whose religious convictions are significantly different from your own? For example, a Jew, Buddhist, or Muslim? Or a fundamentalist Christian if you are not, or vice versa?

What is most important here, I think, is to be respectful, and to accept people exactly where they are. When I succeed in conveying respect, people let down their guard and become more respectful of what I might have to say. And I almost always find much that I can easily respect in people's ways of thinking and being.

I look for what we hold in common. Usually we hold in common what is most important: the meaningfulness of human existence and the primacy of love. With the exception of most Buddhists, we also hold in common a belief in a loving God. I lay most of my emphasis on that common ground, and it is sufficiently substantive to permit all that I want to do in therapy with the spiritual dimension.

It is a common principle in therapy to go with and build on the worldview the client brings. This applies also to the client's spiritual beliefs. Wherever possible, I use their language and build on beliefs I hear them articulate. The one exception is when I judge it useful to challenge a belief I see to be harmful. The best way to do this is to ground the challenge in an even larger or deeper belief we hold in common, such as the goodness of God or the primacy of love.

If I sensed that a client and I were clashing spiritually, and our differences were producing more tension than anything else, I would apologize for not having been sufficiently respectful of their beliefs, and after that I would simply stop raising spiritual considerations or reacting to theirs. So far, I have not had this experience.

4. Do you pray with clients?

I pray with any client who expresses a desire to pray. Some like to open the session with a prayer, or end with one.

I suggest we pray whenever I feel so moved, telling the client why I feel so moved and checking to see if they want to pray. In the actual praying either of us might do the verbal expression, or both of us, or neither, as sometimes we just share a prayerful silence.

The usefulness of praying together is to make explicit the faith we share and the context in which we are working, to give expression to what we are feeling or hoping for, and to ask God's help.

Every morning, I pray for each of the people I am going to see that day, holding them up to God and asking God to make me an instrument of grace and healing for them. In sessions when I am guiding someone through an internal exercise such as focusing or visualization, I always support them silently with prayer.[2]

But just as I do not mention God in every session, there are many sessions in which I do not pray with or for the client. Again, I tend to assume that we already share a context of faith. I believe that God, who knows far better than either of us exactly what we need (Mt

6:32), and who is always laboring with us and for us, is already quietly at work in this situation. In fact, when I am asked where I find God
in my life, one of the first places I name is the counseling setting. For
me it is a genuinely sacred place, because in it two persons, each an
embodiment of God, in trust and mutual love, are talking about the
experiences and underlying meanings of human existence. That is a
sacred event. I see it as the sort of setting Jesus envisioned when he
said, "Where two or three are gathered in my name, there I am in the
midst of them" (Mt 18:20).

5. Is there a Christian psychotherapy?

Yes and no, but mostly no. First, there are a great many schools or
modes of psychotherapy, and a Christian therapist might espouse any
one of them, or use a combination of them, as I do myself. Some may
be more congenial to a Christian point of view than others, but I think
all of them contain insights and techniques a Christian therapist can
use. There are also a great many spiritualities—Jewish, Christian,
Buddhist, to name a few—and so a therapy might be spiritual without
being Christian. What makes a therapy spiritual is the bringing of
spiritual considerations into the therapeutic process. Then, that larger
and deeper context within which therapy rests is brought to conscious
awareness and more fully tapped as a resource. When the spirituality
is from the Jesus tradition, the spirituality is Christian. But then,
rather than saying a Christian psychotherapy is being employed, I
would say a Christian psychotherapist is using Christian spirituality as
framework and resource for the therapy.

6. How much spirituality or theology do I have to know before I am competent to use Christian spirituality in doing therapy?

The more theology you know, the better off you are. But of course it
is not mere head knowledge. The more you live a Christian spirituality and understand what you are living, the more competent and confi-
dent you will be in using it to assist others.

    The ideal situation for clients who wish to integrate the spiritual
into their therapy is that the therapist have a better grasp of spirituality
and its applications to life situations than the client does, so that the

therapist really has something to offer in the spiritual as well as in the psychological realm. But considerably less than that can be quite helpful. Something any therapist can do is ask a thought-provoking question: "Does your faith or your spirituality have anything to say about this situation?" That allows and encourages the integration, putting the focus on the client.[3] Some obvious points of insertion for such a question are occasions when what therapist Irwin Yalom calls "the existential questions" lurk in the background of the discussion and give rise to basic anxiety: death, the meaning of life, one's freedom, and the experience of aloneness.[4] There are other times, too, when an implicit cry for a deeper resource can be heard. So a therapist who sees the relevance of the spiritual, even though he or she does not feel particularly well schooled, can at least ask the question which brings the spiritual into awareness.

Another useful thing a therapist can do is share a personal experience coming out of their own spiritual frame. "I know when I am dealing with something like this, it helps me to realize...." That points up the relevance of the spiritual, joins with the client's faith, and sets the client thinking along spiritual lines.

I am suggesting that even small touches can be very helpful, and they do not require a particularly rich personal theology or spirituality. Naturally, the more deeply immersed one is in theology and spirituality, the more resourceful one can be. What the therapist most wants to avoid is showing no respect for the client's spirituality, as if it were all so much illusion or irrelevance. Or being respectful, but obviously feeling so inadequate and therefore uncomfortable when the topic comes up that the client comes to the rescue of the therapist and stops mentioning it, regretful nevertheless that such an important part of their life is being left out of consideration.

7. What spiritual resources would be most helpful to me as a therapist?

I would name familiarity with scripture as the single most useful resource. All Christians regard scripture as the source book of their spirituality and the ultimate norm by which they try to live. Particularly important is the New Testament, with its sayings and stories of Jesus and the theology of Paul. The best way to gain familiarity with scripture is by repeated reading and meditation on its texts.

Over and above scripture, the Christian tradition is rich in theologians, mystics, prophets, and countless holy women and men whose writings and stories offer immense insight and inspiration. Courses, workshops, talks, retreats, and personal reading all provide access to this treasury.

But obviously what is needed is more than the command of a body of knowledge. Personal assimilation is crucial. The effort to cultivate a relationship with God in one's own life, and to live the teachings of Jesus, are indispensable for lending authenticity to a therapist's words about Christian spirituality. In fact, the therapist's whole presence, manner of relating, and approach to therapy can reasonably be expected to exhibit something of his or her spiritual life. I am reminded of an ancient story from the Orient.

> *Disciple:* What is the difference between knowledge and enlightenment?

> *Master:* When you have knowledge, you use a torch to show the way. When you are enlightened, you become a torch.

In working on one's spiritual growth, it is very helpful to walk with a good spiritual guide.

8. What is the difference between spiritual direction, pastoral counseling, and psychotherapy?

Let me begin my answer on a personal note. As a Jesuit priest, I was "spiritual director" to many people. During those years I also worked in parishes, schools, and retreat houses as a "pastoral counselor." These last fifteen years, I have been a "psychotherapist." But I think I have always done pretty much the same thing: I have listened to people with care, and given them my honest responses. It was their lives people have brought me, however they saw my role. They brought whatever most concerned them. And my responses have always come out of an ever growing fund of personal experience, faith convictions, and psychological knowledge. So for me, there has been no major difference among these three practices.

I have also been the seeker rather the provider of help, and from that, too, I have learned something about the relationship of spiritual direction and therapy. I never sought the services of a therapist, but I have received many years of spiritual direction. As I look back over that experience, I can see that that was also my therapy, and I needed it. None of my spiritual directors were therapists or even certified pastoral counselors—with the exception of the priest/psychologist who guided me through my year of decision. But they were all therapists to me. By that I mean that they contributed greatly to my healing and personal growth. They did this simply by providing me a climate in which I could unfold, listening with care to my story, giving me common sense feedback, loving me, encouraging me, challenging and stretching me, and reflecting me back to myself as a person whose life was worth living. I do not know what more the most skilled therapist could do. I could describe the benefits I derived all in purely psychological terms, yet the work was all done under the aegis of growth in the Christian life. And from this I conclude that good spiritual direction is also good therapy.[5] My experience brings to mind the words of veteran therapist (psychiatrist) Irwin Yalom, who remarks of therapy:

> Over the years I've learned that the therapist's venture is not to engage the patient in a joint archeological dig. If any patients have ever been helped in that fashion, it wasn't because of the search and the finding of that false trail (a life never goes wrong because of a false trail; it goes wrong because the main trail is false). No, a therapist helps a patient not by sifting through the past but by being lovingly present with that person; by being trustworthy, interested; and by believing that their joint activity will ultimately be redemptive and healing. The drama of age regression and incest recapitulation (or, for that matter, any therapeutic cathartic or intellectual project) is healing only because it provides therapist and patient with some interesting shared activity while the real therapeutic force—the relationship—is ripening on the tree.[6]

What Yalom says of therapy seems to me true also of spiritual direction. The relationship itself, when it is a good one, is therapeutic.

What I do today is called therapy. But I consider all my therapy also spiritual direction. This is because I bring the spiritual dimension into it, taking people where they are and helping them foster their spiritual growth by discerning and responding to the presence and invitation of God in the concern they bring. For I believe God is where the action is, and now is the opportune moment. In Paul's words, "This is the acceptable time; now is the day of salvation" (2 Cor 6:2).

So with regard to the question about the difference between the three endeavors, perhaps more depends on who is doing them than on whatever each of them might be described as in the abstract. I think the Christian helper who has adequate grounding in psychology and spirituality is always doing something of all three together. I can imagine a situation in which that Christian helper, presented with a particular spiritual dilemma or question, might say, "That is beyond my competence. I think you need to consult an experienced spiritual director on that." Or, the same Christian helper, presented with bizarre psychic phenomena or behavior, might say: "This is beyond my competence. I think you need to consult an experienced psychotherapist." But in the broad middle ground where most clients live most of the time, this Christian helper actually combines the three endeavors and is competent to do so. What of the psychotherapist who has no interest in the spiritual dimension, particularly when with the client who has no interest in it either? Well, we could hardly call what they do together pastoral counseling or spiritual direction. It is simply therapy. And yet even there, on theological principles developed earlier, I believe that God is present and active in what they are doing for all the good that can be brought out of it for each of them.

Perhaps a good way to differentiate among these three endeavors with their extensive overlap is to think in terms of what the client is seeking, and what the helper has in the way of training and experience. This is what determines the proportions of the ingredients.

In my experience, people seek out a spiritual director when they want to bring their whole lives more into harmony with God. What they have in mind is an ongoing relationship with a spiritual guide over time, to support their personal/spiritual growth. They will sometimes bring religious experiences, to test whether they are valid and discuss what their implications might be. They will sometimes talk about their prayer, especially if they are experiencing difficulty. But much more often, they will talk about day-to-day life, bringing whatever pains or puzzles them, looking for direction as to how a God-seeking person ought to handle these things. What they want in the director is a caring person who has some expertise in matters spiritual. And that is indeed the core of the spiritual director's training and experience. What they also want, though they may not as fully realize it, is someone who has at least a layperson's grasp of ordinary psychodynamics and human relationships, a person who is balanced and solidly grounded in the real world, because in the hands of a different sort of person spirituality can be a dangerous thing.

People seek out a pastoral counselor (most often, the priest or minister in their church) when some problem is bothering them, and they want help with it from someone who shares their faith. These clients are problem-focused, and envision a time-limited relationship, sometimes even just a single conversation. The shared faith is crucial for them. It inspires trust in the integrity of the helper, and also gives assurance that the helper views the problem in the context of the ultimate meaning, purpose, and values of the person's life. They do not think of the pastoral counselor as deeply trained in psychology, but they presume he or she has some psychological training and considerable life and counseling experience, and so is a wise and good advisor. And this is usually a fair assessment of what the pastoral counselor is. There is a new type of pastoral counselor in our day, one who has far deeper grounding in psychology and sometimes also additional theology, and who typically works in a pastoral counseling center rather than a church. This person's expertise qualifies him or her as a psychotherapist, which is our next category of helper.[7]

People seek out a psychotherapist when some problem is bothering them, and they want help with it from someone with expertise in the psychological realm. It may be a present crisis which prompts them to seek help. Or it may be ongoing distress or unhappiness in their lives, and they are concerned that their problem may be deep-seated psychologically. The psychotherapist's training and experience lie precisely in the psychological realm. Therapy may take a long time, or it may be relatively brief. The spiritual dimension may or may not be important to the client. If it is, they may seek out the specially trained pastoral counselor, or they may ask the psychotherapist on the phone: "Are you a Christian therapist?" Then it is especially important that the therapist integrate the spiritual into the therapy.

I have differentiated the three undertakings here primarily in terms of what the client is seeking and what the helper is trained and experienced in. These factors determine the proportions of psychology and spirituality in the dialogue as well as their quality. Frequently both are present. And it seems to me that both always have a crucial role to play if we want to deal therapeutically with the totality of the human person.

9. How would you compare your thought on these matters with that of others in the field?

Let me answer this by very briefly summarizing and commenting on the thought of three prominent writers in the field: psychiatrist/spiritual director Gerald May, pastoral counselor Robert Wicks, and psychotherapist/spiritual director Thomas Moore.

Gerald May distinguishes quite sharply between psychotherapy and spiritual direction. He calls them "fundamentally different undertakings,"[8] and pinpoints the difference in terms of content and intent.

May says the intent of therapy is to "bolster an individual's capacity to gratify needs and desires and to achieve a sense of autonomous mastery over self and circumstance," whereas spiritual direction "seeks liberation from attachments and a self-giving surrender to the discerned power and will of God."[9] In terms of content, May says therapy is concerned with "mental and emotional dimensions (thoughts, feelings, moods, and so on)," while spiritual direction "focuses more precisely on spiritual issues such as prayer life, religious experiences, and sense of relationship to God."[10]

I see therapy and spiritual direction as more similar and overlapping, as chapter 2 in particular draws out, and this whole book attempts to demonstrate. Always I think it is the whole person the helper is dealing with, and therefore the person's whole life that comes under discussion (content). And always I think the helping project is directed toward healing, liberation, growth, fulfillment (intent). May shows well that certain kinds of therapy can be too limited in focus, and might even promote willfulness and selfishness rather than true human fulfillment. He does not show a corresponding wariness of the pitfalls of certain kinds of spirituality. But I agree with him in his insistence that people need a healthy spirituality to help them ground their lives in the deepest values and truest perspectives.

I suspect there are two reasons why Gerald May and I at least seem to diverge so much. One is that I started as a spiritual director, saw the usefulness of psychology to what I was doing, and gradually incorporated more and more of it into my spiritual framework. Gerald May started as a psychiatrist, experienced the limits of what psychiatry could do, turned to the study of spirituality and began to do spiritual direction. Having gone that route, one might very well be inclined to think, "This is the real answer to what people need, and psychiatry does not hit it at all." Then one might see them as very distinct endeavors, and view the spiritual approach as vastly superior. The second reason is an apparent difference in our theological starting points. I think May more sharply differentiates between secular and sacred. Mine is an Ignatian, incarnational theology which sees the secular as suffused with the sacred, and finds God in all things.

Robert Wicks, a pastoral counselor, is another person who has written extensively of the relationship between therapy, pastoral counseling, and spiritual direction. He demarcates the territories of each by their "content or focus of concern":

Psychotherapy ("secular counseling"): person's relationship with him/herself and the world.

Pastoral counseling: person's relationship with him/herself and others with an eye to the influence God has in his/her everyday life.

Spiritual direction: person's relationship with God.[11]

What Wicks describes as the domain of pastoral counseling, I see as a very accurate description of what I have been calling spiritual direction! We may simply be using different terms for the same project. I like his description's inclusiveness: relationships with self, others, and God. I would probably add "the world" as a fourth relationship, as he does under "psychotherapy." In other words, the person's whole life is under discussion in what I call "spiritual direction" and he calls "pastoral counseling," and in all of the person's life a harmonious relationship with God is being sought. Wicks' "pastoral counselor" has more training in psychology than many spiritual directors do (not all), and so will probably be richer in psychological resourcefulness.

Wicks' description of the domain of "spiritual direction" sounds a little impoverished. If spiritual direction talked only about a person's relationship with God, it would very quickly run out of things to talk about. It must also discuss how the person relates to self, others, and the world, not only because these relationships constitute so much of any human life, but because each of us lives out our relationship with God precisely in these other relationships. Even the most spiritual person never "rises above" the world and has to do only with God; we have always to deal with the world because we are situated in it. As Karl Rahner put it, we are incarnate spirit, or spirit-in-the-world. This is what Wicks shows such a good sense of in his description of "pastoral counseling."

In his book *Care of the Soul*,[12] psychotherapist/spiritual director Thomas Moore contrasts psychotherapy with what he thinks is really needed by people today—care of the soul. He holds that psychotherapy is too taken up with curing—fixing, changing, adjusting, making healthy, trying to achieve a trouble-free existence. Moore calls for the "re-imagining" of psychotherapy so that it includes spirituality and attends more to care than cure. People today complain of emptiness, he says, of meaninglessness, vague depression, loss of values, yearning for personal fulfillment. Such symptoms are indicative of loss of soul. Moore declines to define soul, but in his descriptions he speaks of genuineness and depth, of value and personal substance, of a quality revealed in attachment, love, and community, as well as in retreat on behalf of inner communing and intimacy.

I like Moore's emphases. Like May, he makes an excellent case for psychotherapy's need of spirituality to complete it. His "symptoms" of our age are precisely the deeper human problems which psychotherapy is incapable of addressing without the help of spirituality.

The only point at which I would qualify Moore is in the sharpness of his contrast between care and cure, and in what sometimes sounds like a denigration of therapy. Sometimes curing is possible, and always the curing of what ails us is good. I believe the first

Christian response to evil—anxiety, depression, migraine headaches, low self-esteem, for example—is to resist and overcome it. This was Jesus' own response to the suffering he saw. Only after we have done all we can do to overcome it should we accept the unsolved remainder with trust in God. I view therapy's resourcefulness in bringing healing to various intrapsychic and interpersonal afflictions as a great assist to spirituality. If spirituality could do it all, the mental health field probably would not have come into existence.

Moore is right is saying there are many human problems we cannot cure, but I would say let us cure the ones we can, with the assurance that our efforts coincide with God's own. I agree with him though that sometimes all the helper can do is walk along with people in their suffering, supporting them in their struggle while God and they bring out of it all possible good. I like his idea of listening carefully for the voice of the soul as people lay out what troubles them.

10. What do you find yourself saying most often to your therapy clients from the fund of your spirituality?

That they are good. That they are loved by God. That their lives are meaningful. That things work out. That God is not out there but right here in the world of their experience. That they are meant for a relationship with God and need God in their lives. That is probably a fair summary of my faith. And it is a saving message—very therapeutic.

Notes

1. The Presence of God in Ordinary Life

[1] Rahner has written voluminously, and the metaphor of the horizon is scattered throughout his works. One place where he develops it at some length is in his treatment of the human person in *Foundations of Christian Faith* (Seabury, 1978), 24–43.

[2] Tillich's metaphor is likewise found throughout his works. He makes it the theme of a provocative sermon in *The Shaking of the Foundations* (Scribner's, 1948), 52–63.

[3] See Rosemary Radford Ruether, *Disputed Questions: On Being a Christian* (Abingdon, 1982), 24.

[4] Sally McFague: *Models of God: Theology for an Ecological, Nuclear Age* (Fortress, 1987), 69–77.

[5] Charlene Spretnak, *States of Grace: The Recovery of Meaning in the Postmodern Age* (Harper, 1991), 136.

[6] Spretnak, *op. cit.*, 133.

Ruether, McFague, Spretnak are all exponents of feminist theology, a contemporary movement of great importance for its commitment to overcoming all the great oppressions: of women, of nature, of certain races, of the poor. Feminism opposes the dualistic mode of thinking which divides reality into polarities and then asserts the superiority of one pole over the other: spirit vs. body, male vs. female, white vs. color, heterosexual vs. homosexual, humanity vs. nature, reason vs. emotion, action vs. contemplation. Feminism thinks holistically or ecologically, extols the rich variety of creation, and emphasizes dignity and interdependence. I am deeply indebted to feminist theology, and recommend the following works as introductions. Carol Christ and Judith Plaskow, eds., have assembled two fine anthologies which show the breadth of its concerns: *Womanspirit Rising* (Harper, 1979), and *Weaving the Visions* (Harper, 1989). A sample of themes from one of feminism's pioneer theologians can be found in Rosemary Radford Ruether, *Sexism and God-Talk* (Beacon, 1983). Kathleen Fischer, *Reclaiming the Connections* (Sheed and Ward, 1989), offers a compelling contemporary spirituality informed by a feminist vision.

[7] The contemporary school known as "process theology" is another major force in promoting an integrated vision, and a major influence on my thought. Stemming from Alfred North Whitehead (1861–1947), this school highlights the primacy of becoming and of relation in our experience of reality. Sometimes called a "philosophy of organism," it emphasizes the vital interconnectedness of all things in an endless process of evolution, with God at the heart of the process. Whitehead, notoriously difficult to read, is perhaps most accessible in his *Science and the Modern World* (Free Press, 1967), or his *Adventures of Ideas* (Free Press, 1967). A fine summary of process theology is John Cobb and David Griffin's *Process Theology* (Westminster, 1976).

The French paleontologist and Jesuit, Pierre Teilhard de Chardin (1881–1955), widely known for his unique personal synthesis of scientific evolutionary thinking and Christian mysticism, is regarded as another source of process theology. Working independently of Whitehead, he portrays a universe charged with the presence and organizing activity of the cosmic Christ. His mystic vision is well conveyed in his *Hymn of the Universe* (Harper, 1969). His two main systematic works are *The Phenomenon of Man* (Harper, 1961) and *The Divine Milieu* (Harper, 1965).

[8] Rudolph Bultmann, *Theology of the New Testament* (Scribner's, 1951), 195.

[9] George E. Ganss, S.J., ed., *Ignatius of Loyola: The Spiritual Exercises and Selected Works* (Paulist, 1991).

2. Psychotherapy and Spirituality

[1] This criticism of therapy is strongly articulated by a group of

prominent sociologists in Robert Bellah et al., *Habits of the Heart* (Univ. of California, 1985), 98–141.

[2] Orbis, 1985.

[3] Vintage, 1965.

[4] See Carl Jung, *Modern Man in Search of a Soul* (Harvest, 1933).

[5] This triple comparison is nicely developed in Richard Kropf, *Faith: Security and Risk* (Paulist, 1990), 5–19.

[6] Viktor Frankl, *Man's Search for Meaning: An Introduction to Logotherapy* (Pocket Books, 1959).

[7] Viktor Frankl, *The Unconscious God: Psychotherapy and Theology* (Simon and Schuster, 1975), 75.

[8] The thought of well-known contemporary existentialist therapist Irwin Yalom comes to mind here. While not necessarily espousing a religious solution, Yalom sees the human person as inevitably grappling with the question of meaning, and sees that issue as therapy's principal focus. "I believe that the primal stuff of psychotherapy is always such existence pain—and not, as is often claimed, repressed instinctual strivings or imperfectly buried shards of a tragic personal past. In my therapy...my primary clinical assumption...is that basic anxiety emerges from a person's endeavors, conscious and unconscious, to cope with the harsh facts of life, the 'givens' of existence. I have found that four givens are particularly relevant to psychotherapy: the inevitability of death for each of us and for those we love; the freedom to make our lives as we will; our ultimate aloneness; and, finally, the absence of any obvious meaning or sense to life. However grim these givens may seem, they contain the seeds of wisdom and redemption." (Irwin Yalom, M.D., *Love's Executioner* [Harper, 1989], 4–5.) Yalom concisely frames the issues which orient the person toward the transcendent.

[9] Abraham Maslow, *Motivation and Personality* (Harper, 1954, revised 1970).

[10] Penguin, 1970.

[11] Maslow, *op. cit.*, 55–6.

[12] Carol Gilligan, *In a Different Voice* (Harvard University Press, 1982). See also Judith Jordan, Alexandra Kaplan, Jean Baker Miller, Irene Stiver, and Janet Surrey, *Women's Growth in Connection: Writings from the Stone Center* (Guilford Press, 1991).

[13] Robert Kegan, *The Evolving Self: Problem and Process in Human Development* (Harvard University Press, 1982).

[14] Psychologist David Richo articulates a very similar position in his *How to Be an Adult: A Handbook on Psychological and Spiritual Integration* (Paulist, 1991).

[15] I am indebted for this line of synthesis to Joann Wolski Conn, *Spirituality and Personal Maturity* (Paulist, 1989).

[16] Gerald May, *Addiction and Grace* (Harper, 1988).

[17] Gerald May, *Will and Spirit* (Harper, 1982), 2.

[18] More exploration along these lines can be found in Reed Payne, Allen Bergin, and Patricia Loftus, "A Review of Attempts to Integrate Spiritual and Standard Psychotherapy Techniques," in *Journal of Psychotherapy Integration*, Vol. 2, No. 3, 1992, 171–92.

[19] For a balanced assessment of the great harm and the great good *all* the major religions have done, see John Hick, "The Non-Absoluteness of Christianity" in John Hick and Paul Knitter, eds., *The Myth of Christian Uniqueness* (Orbis, 1987).

[20] Albert Ellis, widely published founder of the school of rational-emotive therapy, calls himself a "probabilistic atheistic humanist" because he sees no clear evidence for God and finds religion frequently an obstacle to human growth. His principal critique of religion is of religious absolutism: "People largely disturb themselves by believing strongly in absolutistic shoulds, oughts, and musts, and most people who dogmatically believe in some religion believe in these health-sabotaging absolutes. The emotionally healthy individual is flexible, open, tolerant, and changing, and the devoutly religious person tends to be inflexible, closed, intolerant, and unchanging. Religiosity, therefore, is in many respects equivalent to irrational thinking and emotional disturbance." (*Journal of Consulting and Clinical Psychology*, 1980, Vol. 48, No. 5, 635–39.)

[21] He writes up his experiences and philosophy in A. S. Neill, *Summerhill: A Radical Approach to Child Rearing* (NY: Hart, 1960).

[22] Neill, *op. cit.*, xxiii.

[23] Neill, *op. cit.*, 356.

[24] Neill, *op. cit.*, 344.

[25] For a fuller discussion, see Paul Knitter, "Toward a Liberation Theology of Religions" in *The Myth of Christian Uniqueness* (Orbis, 1987); and Hans Kung, "What Is True Religion? Toward an Ecumenical Criteriology" in Leonard Swidler, ed., *Toward a Universal Theology of Religion* (Orbis, 1987).

[26] Rosemary Radford Ruether, *Sexism and God-Talk* (Beacon, 1983), 24.

[27] Ruether, *op. cit.*, 19.

3. Toward a Healthy Spirituality: Ten Guiding Principles

[1] Edward Schillebeeckx, *Jesus: An Experiment in Christology* (Crossroad, 1979), 140–54.

[2] For a fine treatment of the problem of evil in the world in the face of God's goodness, see Harold Kushner, *When Bad Things Happen to Good People* (Schocken Books, 1981); William P. Roberts, "God and Prayer When You're Suffering," in *Praying*, No. 19, July-August 1987, 4; Wendy Farley, *Tragic Vision and Divine Compassion: A Contemporary Theodicy* (Westminster, 1990).

[3] This line of thinking on the death of Jesus can be found more fully developed in many recent works on Christology; for example, Jon Sobrino, *Christology at the Crossroads* (Orbis, 1976); Albert Nolan, *Jesus before Christianity* (Orbis, 1978); Thomas Hart, *To Know and Follow Jesus* (Paulist, 1984); Marcus Borg, *Jesus: A New Vision* (Harper, 1987).

[4] For a fuller discussion of the richness of biblical imagery, the danger of idolatry, and the advantages of bringing lesser used images into play, see Sally McFague, *Models of God* (Fortress, 1987), Virginia Ramey Mollenkott, *The Divine Feminine* (Crossroad, 1984),

or Elizabeth Johnson, *She Who Is: The Mystery of God in Feminist Theological Discourse* (Crossroad, 1992).

[5] See Wilkie Au, *By Way of the Heart* (Paulist, 1989), 67.

[6] For a fine summary of Whitehead's thought on God's creative love as persuasive and as interested in promoting creaturely enjoyment, see John Cobb and David Griffin, *Process Theology* (Westminster, 1976), 52–57.

[7] For a fuller elaboration of these ideas, see my book on spiritual direction: Thomas Hart, *The Art of Christian Listening* (Paulist, 1980), chapters 7 and 8.

[8] See the "Rules for the Discernment of Spirits" in George E. Ganss, S.J., ed., *Ignatius of Loyola: The Spiritual Exercises and Selected Works* (Paulist, 1991), 201–07.

4. The Man Who Hated Himself

[1] A helpful book on the cause of psychological breakdown, the treatment of it, and the prevalence of religious symbolism in what the subject recounts after the break, is John Weir Perry's *The Far Side of Madness* (Prentice Hall, 1974).

[2] Carl Jung, *Memories, Dreams, and Reflections* (Vintage, 1965), ch. 1–2.

5. Battling Depression

[1] John McNeill, *The Church and the Homosexual* (revised, Beacon, 1988), in which he discusses the moral issues; and *Taking a Chance on God: Spirituality for Gays and Lesbians* (Beacon, 1988), in which he offers a rich spirituality specifically for gays and lesbians.

[2] See David Burns, *Feeling Good* (Signet, 1980).

[3] For the rationale of visualization and a variety of guided exercises, see Marlene Halpin, *Imagine That!: Using Phantasy in Spiritual Direction* (Dubuque: William C. Brown Co., 1982), or Adelaide Bry with Marjorie Bair, *Visualization: Directing the Movies of Your Mind* (Harper, 1978).

[4] Anthony de Mello, *Awareness* (Doubleday, 1990). Like other eastern masters (though this one also happens to be a Catholic priest), de Mello imparts his wisdom through stories. Two of his collections are *The Song of the Bird* (Loyola University Press, 1983), and *Taking Flight* (Doubleday, 1988).

6. Is This Marriage Over?

[1] For a practical book on how to make marriage work, which at the same time weaves in the spirituality of marriage, see Kathleen Fischer and Thomas Hart, *Promises to Keep: Developing the Skills of Marriage* (Paulist, 1992).

[2] For a fine treatment of how a faith perspective can help us bear loss as well as face the other difficulties of life, see Charles Verge, "Foundations for a Spiritually Based Psychotherapy," in Laurel Burton, ed., *Religion and the Family* (NY: Haworth Press, 1992), 41–59.

7. How Could God Allow This?

[1] Full references to both books are given in the footnotes of chapter 3.

[2] Douglas Anderson shows a wonderful sense of these mysterious workings of grace as he describes doing therapy with couples and families in "Spirituality and Systems Therapy: Partners in Clinical Practice," in Laurel Burton, ed., *Religion and the Family* (Haworth, 1992), 87–101.

8. The Woman Who Was Selfish

[1] I have attempted to deal with this and a host of other issues where the psychological and spiritual cross over in daily life in a small book designed as a retreat follow-up, Thomas Hart, *Coming Down the Mountain: How to Turn Your Retreat into Everyday Living* (Paulist, 1988).

[2] A wonderful resource for women in battling sexist conditioning on both psychological and spiritual grounds is Kathleen Fischer's

Women at the Well: Feminist Perspectives on Spiritual Direction (Paulist, 1988).

[3] For this approach I am significantly indebted to Eugene Gendlin, *Focusing* (Bantam, 1981).

9. Who Am I—Really?

[1] My biblical studies later persuaded me that God never did want Abraham to sacrifice Isaac, but that Abraham *thought* God wanted the sacrifice of Isaac. He thought that because religious people of his time and place made a regular practice of infant sacrifice, thinking thereby that they pleased God as they understood God. The whole point of the story is the changing of that God-image.

[2] The Greek term of the gospel saying, *psyche*, means both soul and self.

[3] Leo has set forth many of his ideas on spirituality in his book, Leo Rock, S.J., *Making Friends with Yourself* (Paulist, 1991).

[4] You will have noticed that four of my "Principles of a Healthy Spirituality" were operative in the experience I recount here. In fact, they crystallized for me in the process. The four:

God wants life for us.
God's will for us is found within our own deepest wanting.
Good people are tempted by what seems morally or spiritually good.
God often appears in human form.

10. Questions about Practice

[1] In the therapy field at large, there is a movement away from the therapist-as-expert, to therapist and client as fellow explorers and collaborators in seeking solutions to human problems. See, for example, Stephen Gilligan and Reese Price, eds., *Therapeutic Conversations* (Norton, 1993).

[2] My wife and I have published a book of prayers and healing rituals for use in counseling situations, as well as prayers for therapists to

use personally in developing their own spiritual life: Kathleen Fischer and Thomas Hart, *A Counselor's Prayerbook* (Paulist, 1994).

[3] People's responses to the question I usually ask, "Where do you think God is in all this?" are fascinating. Here is a sample:

1) Total silence and a puzzled face, indicating bafflement. I like it. I made them think.

2) (Embarrassed) "Interesting that you should mention that. I haven't been going to church lately. I don't pray as much as I should either." This is the one I get most often. It suggests that the person feels out of contact with God, and would have to get back to church to renew that contact. They probably think this is what I am suggesting. I am not.

3) "I don't know, but I know that God is always with me." Nice answer. It indicates a live faith, integrated into daily existence. All it lacks is specificity about how God might be using this particular struggle.

4) A brief, thoughtful silence, and then the product of that moment's reflection. For example, "I suppose God is asking me to love my husband in spite of what he's done." Bingo! This person sees the situation itself as having spiritual significance. A better answer may follow more reflection, but they are right on line.

[4] Irwin Yalom, *Love's Executioner* (Harper, 1989), 4–5.

[5] I have written a book on spiritual direction, which grew out of my experience in training others how to do it. See Thomas Hart, *The Art of Christian Listening* (Paulist, 1980).

[6] Irwin Yalom, *Love's Executioner* (Harper, 1989), 227.

[7] Today's "pastoral counselor" strictly so-called, often has at least a master's degree in psychology and counseling, sometimes a Ph.D., belongs to a professional association which oversees standards and credentialing (e.g., American Association of Pastoral Counselors), and works in a counseling center, charging fees comparable to those charged by other mental health professionals. Because of this recent development in the pastoral field, at least one writer on pastoral counseling seeks to promote clarity by distinguishing "pastoral care" (practically everything a pastor does), "pastoral counseling" (counsel-

ing by a pastor with ordinary pastoral training), and "pastoral psychotherapy" (counseling or therapy by a pastor with extensive training in psychotherapy). See Donald S. Browning, "Introduction to Pastoral Counseling," in Robert J. Wicks, Richard D. Parsons, and Donald Capps, eds., *Clinical Handbook of Pastoral Counseling*, Vol. 1 (Paulist, 1993), 5–13.

Interestingly, in his *Taking on the Gods: The Task of the Pastoral Counselor* (Abingdon, 1986), Merle Jordan sounds a note of warning to his fellow pastoral psychotherapists: We can become so fascinated with our psychological expertise that we abdicate spirituality in favor of doing straight psychotherapy. When we do, we disappoint our clients and lose our greatest therapeutic resource.

[8] Gerald May, *Care of Mind/Care of Spirit* (Harper, 1982), 12.

[9] *Op. cit.*, 14.

[10] *Op. cit.*, 13.

[11] Robert Wicks, *Self-Ministry through Self-Understanding* (Chicago: Loyola University Press, 1983), 12.

[12] Thomas Moore, *Care of the Soul* (HarperCollins, 1992).

Suggestions for Further Reading

Au, Wilkie. *By Way of the Heart: Toward a Holistic Christian Spirituality.* Mahwah, N.J.: Paulist Press, 1989. An experienced counselor and spiritual guide shows how psychology and religion can be natural allies in the process by which we are made whole and holy. Written from the same conviction, Wilkie Au and Noreen Cannon's *Urgings of the Heart: A Spirituality of Integration* (Mahwah, N.J.: Paulist Press, 1995) explores concrete human struggles, such as codependency, envy, perfectionism, overwork, and intimacy.

Becvar, Dorothy Stroh. *Soul Healing: A Spiritual Orientation in Counseling and Therapy.* New York: Basic Books, 1997. An established author in the fields of spirituality, therapy, and family offers a treatment of spirituality and healing in general and then of clinical strategies for dealing with various counseling issues.

Fischer, Kathleen. *Transforming Fire: Women Using Anger Creatively.* Mahwah, N.J.: Paulist Press, 1999. Written specifically for women, though well-suited to both genders, this is a psychological/spiritual treatment of the knotty issues surrounding anger, e.g., anger's disguises, conflict, violence, resistance, forgiveness, and action for change.

Fischer, Kathleen, and Thomas Hart. *A Counselor's Prayerbook.* Mahwah, N.J.: Paulist Press, 1994. A collection of prayers and healing rituals for counselors and counselees.

Griffith, James and Melissa. *Encountering the Sacred in Psychotherapy.* New York: Guilford, 2002. Teaches therapists how to engage in conversations about spirituality in therapy. Topics include whether and when to raise spiritual issues, how to talk about God, how to deal with belief systems, how to dialogue about religious convictions that may seem destructive. Includes case examples.

Miller, William R., ed. *Integrating Spirituality into Treatment: Resources for Practitioners.* New York: American Psychological Association, 1999. A collection of essays addressing broad aspects of spirituality, including acceptance, forgiveness, hope, values, and control. Affirms the importance of spirituality in sound psychological practice.

Palmer, Michael. *Freud and Jung on Religion.* New York: Routledge, 1997. Analyzes and critiques the thought of these two seminal and differently persuaded psychotherapists on the relevance of religion to psychotherapy.

Plante, Thomas, and Allen Sherman, eds. *Faith and Health: Psychological Perspectives.* New York: Guilford, 2001. A collection of essays exploring links between spirituality and mental and physical health. Deals with such issues as mortality, aging, forgiveness, cancer, AIDS, tobacco and alcohol use, and healing.

Richards, P. Scott, and Allen Bergin, eds. *A Spiritual Strategy for Counseling and Psychotherapy.* Washington D.C.: American Psychological Association, 1997. Provides guidance for integrating a theistic spiritual strategy into mainstream approaches to psychology and psychotherapy. Summarizing the evolution of psychotherapy, and including case studies, the book puts a theistic strategy on a parallel path with the more traditional forms of psychotherapy. See also their *Handbook of Psychotherapy and Religious Diversity* (Washington, D.C.: American Psychological Association, 1999), which summarizes the core beliefs of Catholics, Protestants, Evangelicals, Mormons, Muslims, Buddhists, Hindus, and the "ethnic-centered spirituality" of blacks, Hispanics, Asian Americans, and American Indians, specifically to increase competency and sensitivity in clinical practice.

Richardson, Peter Tufts. *Four Spiritualities: Expressions of Self, Expressions of Spirit.* Palo Alto, Calif.: Davies-Black, 1996. Stresses the importance of matching one of the four basic paths present in each of the world's great spiritual traditions with a client's Jungian personality type as delineated by Myers-Briggs. The four spiritualities are the Journey of Unity, of Devotion, of Works, and of Harmony.

Smith, C. Michael. *Psychotherapy and the Sacred: Religious Experience and Religious Resources in Psychotherapy.* Chicago: Center for the Scientific Study of Religion, 1995. Pleads for the restoration of religious perspectives in working with mental illness in therapy and in rituals, with case studies.

Walsh, Froma, ed. *Spiritual Resources in Family Therapy.* New York: Guilford Press, 1999. Essays with a focus on the family, exploring spirituality as a sustaining resource for family life and a special help in coping with trauma, poverty, and other suffering.

Wicks, Robert, Richard Parsons, and Donald Capps, eds. *The Clinical Handbook of Pastoral Counseling.* 2 vols. Mahwah, N.J.: Paulist Press, 1985, 1993. A collection of essays on general aspects of psychological/spiritual counseling as well as on specific problems such as addiction, grief, mental illness, marital problems, abuse, depression, PTSD. See also Robert Wicks, ed., *Handbook of Spirituality for Ministers* (2 vols.; Mahwah, N.J.: Paulist Press, 1995, 2000), a practical handbook covering topics for a wider range of persons involved in pastoral care.

Willows, David, and John Swinton, eds. *The Spiritual Dimension of Pastoral Care.* New York: Jessica Kingsley, 2000. A collection of essays by researchers and practitioners critically exploring the way spirituality enters into constructive dialogue with other disciplines and ways of thinking, including psychology and counseling.

Yalom, Irvin, M.D. *The Gift of Therapy.* New York: HarperCollins, 2002. An experienced therapist, trained in psychoanalysis but converted by experience into an existentialist therapist, offers some eighty-five practical suggestions for making counseling sessions more fruitful. He particularly stresses genuineness in the relationship and the importance of getting to the deeper issues beneath a client's particular concerns—questions of meaning, mortality, loneliness, and freedom, i.e., the spiritual issues, though Yalom espouses no faith. He illustrates his convictions in two good novels with therapy at their core: *When Nietzsche Wept* (New York: HarperPerennial, 1993) and *Lying on the Couch* (New York: HarperCollins, 1997).